THE FORTUNES OF THE HUMANITIES

STANFORD UNIVERSITY PRESS
STANFORD, CALIFORNIA

THE FORTUNES OF THE HUMANITIES

Sander L. Gilman

THOUGHTS FOR AFTER THE YEAR 2000

Stanford University Press
Stanford, California

© 2000 by the Board of Trustees of the
Leland Stanford Junior University

Printed in the United States of America

CIP data appear at the end of the book

For the students in all fields

and all places I have taught

and who have taught me

for the past thirty years

CONTENTS

PREFACE

These essays reflect a number of problems that I have confronted in thirty years of teaching the humanities. I am a professor of Germanic studies, but I also have been a teacher of interdisciplinary studies to undergraduate, graduate, and professional students at universities in a number of countries. At the University of Chicago I hold a chair in interdisciplinary medical and humanistic studies; I am the Henry R. Luce Distinguished Service Professor of the Liberal Arts in Human Biology and professor of Germanic studies, comparative literature, and psychiatry as well as a member of the Fishbein Center for the History of Science, the Committee on Jewish Studies, and the Committee on the History of Culture. These essays are the fruits of my concerns as a teacher and a researcher—from the pragmatics of how one uses the classroom to questions of what academic publishing is all about.

German studies has been transformed radically since I was a graduate student in the 1960s. Some of what I write reflects the oddities of a field that has become marginal to many of the concerns of the academy at the end of the millennium, but this very slide into marginality makes it a case study for the problems of teaching and researching the humanities today. My position on the questions I address is clear, even in cases where clarity may render my view too radical or not radical enough for many of my colleagues.

Mine is an unusual generation of academics. I was the first of my family to graduate from high school in the United States and the first to go to university—a great private American institution of higher education, Tulane University. I was admitted at the age of sixteen, I later learned, as a "wild card," because one of the members of the admissions committee saw some academic promise, and I was granted a full scholarship and loans. Had I not been, I would have gone to work straight out of high school, like so many of my friends, and remained solidly within the working class. But as luck had it I was able to move from blue-collar to white-collar employment. Likewise, my graduate work was done under the drive to compete with the Soviets after Sputnik through the National Defense Education Act. Another fluke of history! Entering the profession when there were still some jobs available, I was able to teach in turn at a Catholic women's college (the now-defunct St. Mary's Dominican), a traditional black private university (Dillard), a large, science-oriented university (Case Western Reserve), then, for over two decades, at an Ivy League school with large public colleges (Cornell), and since 1994 at the University of Chicago. My trajectory is not unusual. My generation reaped the benefit of the democratization of the academy with the GI Bill. What we have been experiencing since the 1970s is a further recalibration of the academy—not its dissolution. And the changes we are now witnessing are certainly not as radical as the opening up of the academy following World War II.

The history of American higher education in this century is not a history of collapses but a history of radical reconceptualizations. We are not sitting in the ruins of an ideal Humboldtian system of education based on pure research and teaching but engaged in the ongoing struggle within that wonderful hybrid, the American university system. Given its history—part theological training ground, part research institution, part finishing school for the sons and daughters of the establishment, part professional school for immigrants and children of immigrants, part language school for new citizens—the American university has been neither static nor formed on a single model. Change, indeed radical change, has always been part of its history. The University of Chicago, which was created as a research university on the German model, added a college fairly early in its history to teach undergraduates, and it has redefined its understanding of "basic education" virtually every decade. And such a change is once again taking place. This is not a new situation, but nevertheless radical change demands the intense and comprehensive attention of all of those engaged in the work of the academy. These essays are part of that engagement.

The cry, from the right as well as from the left, has been that one of the great systems of higher education is in danger of collapse. It is clear that the reduction of funds from all sources for American higher education is dramatically shrinking the size of the professoriate. Fewer full-time teachers are being hired; departments and programs in the modern languages and English are in danger of reduction or even closure. While such changes seem in line with downsizing in the early 1990s throughout private industry and the various levels of government, the effect on higher education will have even greater, unforeseen, long-term consequences for the social and economic fabric of the United States.

One of the unintended side effects of the changes in higher education, and one from which I clearly benefited, was a form of affirmative action that encouraged social mobility through education. Through the elimination or reduction of official programs of affirmative action for underrepresented minorities and women, the function of the university as an engine of social change has been altered. But this effect has been exacerbated by the spiraling costs for higher education, even at public institutions, and the tighter limits on the number of truly economically disadvantaged students who can attend. This may well be the most significant change in American higher education over the past ten years.

Higher education in the humanities has been a central part of the creation of an evolving middle class. It has created an educated class which is knowledgeable in ethical and ideological issues, which can read and write critically, which can speak more than one language and therefore participate in a broader world. With the pressures on the system to cut back—to provide less funding for students, to weed on the basis not of merit but of wealth—this system of social mobility is breaking down. (This trend can be best seen in the competition of some schools for the "cream" of each high school class. More money is put toward supporting smaller and smaller numbers of students. The marginal student from the marginal high school who might well flourish in a good university is eliminated from the pool.)

We are also in danger of losing the next generation of university teachers, who will abandon their search for faculty positions and perhaps not even consider studying for doctorates. This will affect every aspect of American society. Students have come and will continue to come to universities for an education that will enable them to achieve a quality of life better than (or at least as good as) that of their parents. Should the university become an upper-middle-class institution with a smattering of marginal students, it will do less and less to alter the social fabric of the United States. Instead it will help perpetuate a permanent underclass without any hope of economic betterment through education. This is the crucial issue of the next decade: not the culture wars, not the canon debate, not the teaching of Shakespeare and/or mass culture. It is the issue that underlies much of this book.

I am extremely grateful to my editor at Stanford University Press, Helen Tartar, who suggested this book and was its most attentive reader. I am also grateful to the audiences that have heard or read versions of these essays and have responded intensely to them.

Several of these essays have appeared elsewhere. The introduction is based on my comments at the November 1997 commencement of the University of Toronto. Chapter 1 originally appeared in *A User's Guide to German Cultural Studies*, ed. Scott Denham et al. (Ann Arbor: University of Michigan Press, 1997), 439–48. Chapter 2 was published in the *University of Toronto Quarterly* 61 (1992): 443–49. Chapter 3 appeared as the MLA Presidential Address 1995, *PMLA* 111 (May 1996): 390–94. Chapter 4 was included in *Germanics under Construction*, ed. Jörg Roche and Thomas Salumets (München: Iudicum, 1996), 9–13. Chapter 7 is based on my keynote address to the Conference on Rethinking German American Writing, Harvard University, September 1998, and chapter 8 on my talk to the incoming class of 2001 of Tulane College, Tulane University, August 1997.

S. L. G.

Chicago, July 1999

THE FORTUNES OF THE HUMANITIES

Introduction

THE FORTUNES

OF THE HUMANITIES

IN AN AGE OF

REALLOCATED

RESOURCES

At the very beginning of his madness, in January 1889, Friedrich Nietzsche attempted to stop a teamster in Turin from beating his horse. He grabbed hold of the horse's neck and, with overwhelming compassion, wept. What would have been an act of civic courage in twentieth-century Toronto was evidently understood as an act of madness in late nineteenth-century Turin. He was treated as a man out of his mind—which of course he was. There and then such tears would have been better wept over the fate of children and the poor than over one of the ubiquitous horses cluttering the streets. Today anyone who weeps about the pitiful state of the humanities in higher education some hundred years after Nietzsche's collapse also runs the risk of being seen as mad.

Yet it is a sign of the new masculinity of our age, of the Million Man Marcher or the Ironman or the Promise Keeper, that a man can weep in public. I weep for the future of the humanities for, like the beaten horse, it seems too trivial a thing to acknowledge, and yet its public debasement is a sign and a portent.

Why weep for the death of the humanities when the social fabric in North America and Western Europe is unraveling and in Eastern Europe it has collapsed? Better to weep for the children without food or housing on the streets of London or New York; for the aged and the sick denied adequate medical care in Stockholm or Bonn; for the migrants shoved from state to state, finding succor in few and solace in none, only the encouragement to "move on" in all; and for the dead and maimed in wars between and among neighbors of all colors, religions, and politics. With so many tears to shed over real calamities, why weep over the decline of the humanities? Indeed, the state of higher education seems too pathetic an object over which to weep, and yet I do, and do so in public.

In the United States after the Second World War, the GI Bill enabled a new generation of scholars to enter the academic world. Many of us entered to explore questions to which we felt the humanities held the answers. There, moral training, the belief that the study of literature or the history of music would make one a better person, had given way to critical thinking, endorsing the view that the study of the humanities would provide students with the tools to analyze and understand their world. Within the university we learned to critique and examine the presuppositions of the world in which we lived rather than to acquire the truths of that world. Theological and social certainty gave way to speculation and analysis. And as we studied and explored, we provided for our students and ourselves precisely the tools needed to understand, in a fragmented and incomplete manner, their world and ours. As literary scholars we trained them (and ourselves) to look at the artifacts of past cultures as well as our own, to dissect them in search of their purposes and complexities. We read poetry with our students; they read the texts of law and medicine using our critical tools.

The system worked. The great humanities scholars of the postwar period came to be engaged in wide-ranging projects as public intellectuals. Their status in the eye of the general public meant that the university system, in which they wrote and taught, respected them. They had honors and status—but perhaps more important, they could undertake their work as public intellectuals because they had *jobs*. These postwar academic intellectuals were, for the most part, members of a generation that would not have had access to higher education had it not been for the GI Bill. Moreover, they were able to address broader and more complex questions because of their status as tenured members of the academic world. They were the product of a new world in which intellectual attainment was not tied to birth or economic status.

That system has begun to close down, both because individuals' access to it is being restricted and because of constant, carping criticism from both ends of the political spectrum. The generation of new knowledge, its transmission, and the social mobility of its students and its teachers—these were the goals of universities from their inception in the Middle Ages and certainly through their revitalization in Humboldt's late Enlightenment idea of the university. The relative decline in economic support for universities in a decade of economic expansion has diminished the role of the university as the place where public debate can and must take place. One sign and consequence of this shift is the use of part-time rather than full-time faculty members to teach, with the concomitant lack of emphasis on the production of knowledge. The dearth of public intellectuals in the academy is a mark of the slide of the status of the university teacher and researcher.

In the world of the *X Files*, I would seek those who destroyed this system and ask why they targeted the teachers of critical thinking and analysis. Did Margaret Thatcher really want to destroy education in the United Kingdom because she was afraid of the democratizing tendencies of the British universities? Was the conscious undercutting of the university system a parallel to her move to institute a poll tax? Did the Republican majority in the American Congress in the mid-1990s, coupled with the weakened leadership of the American universities, deliberately seek to cripple higher education in a time of unprecedented economic growth? Does the federal administration of the Australian university system really believe that stripping academics of the ability to undertake creative research aids the university? Is there an international conspiracy to destroy higher education? Certainly not. But it is clear that all of these moves against higher education stem from ideological positions that seek to weaken or remove the power of higher education to promote social mobility and to serve as a place of active criticism and analysis.

There is no worldwide conspiracy at the universities and against the humanities, for conspiracies are active, and the gradual erosion of the status of the humanities has been a passive undertaking. To be brutal about it, the humanities seem today much too unimportant to warrant such a conspiracy. What we do is not unimportant. But we are now less visible, and there may lie part of the problem. Our invisibility is the result of an interplay of several events and attitudes. Our goals, the goals of the students and teachers and administrators, have become a muddle, and we are *all* at fault for our loss of visibility.

Teachers are at fault because we have lost sight of the goal of our profession, which should be the clear and direct transmission of our critical thinking and complex knowledge even to those who may not immediately benefit from it. Attacks on research in the humanities as "useless" are an attack on the humanities itself. No such attacks are made against the social sciences or natural sciences. Indeed, the funding of certain aspects of science labeled as applied (such as by the National Institutes of Health) is higher than ever, even if the "science" is abstract or basic science. As humanists, we must teach not only our disciples but also the entire world. This may require different means of transmitting knowledge. The oft-bemoaned death of the scholarly book may eventually oblige us to communicate our methods and ideas in other forms to other audiences. "Science writing" is now a standard journalistic specialty; what about the "translation" of our work into forms that could be more easily interpreted by a general readership or audience? The Modern Language Association's widely heard series on National Public Radio is indicative of such an outreach project. In fall 1998, the *New York Times's* creation of an "Arts and Ideas" section in its Saturday edition offered further proof that such an effort is both possible and needed. We have been unable to explain to the "real world" what we do and why we do it; we have been unwilling to become engaged in the dirty fights—the protection of public speech or government funding for humanities and the arts—because we are too good for them. When school systems cut second-language instruction, just as when they cut the arts, we are too often silent. And when university administrators ask us to rethink what we are doing, our answer is too often, "Leave me alone. I must go on doing what I am doing or else the sky will fall."

Students are at fault because they want social mobility without the necessary apprenticeship to learning and the acquisition and generation of knowledge. They should ask not "What use is studying this?" but, rather, "How can I use this?" They have a vital role in the university—not merely in supplying the budget but also in creating the environment in which ideas are tested and methods improved. The university is both classroom and laboratory for the humanities. There methods and ideas are tested—and often found wanting by the students. Then, back to the drawing board!

Administrators are at fault because they want to have an economically viable structure in a world in which value is often measured by a cost/benefit ratio. William Bennett, the conservative guru and former secretary of education under Ronald Reagan, decried the constant rise in university tuition in testimony before the Senate on October 29, 1997. Bennett himself has been a constant and corrosive critic of the National Endowment for the Humanities. His solution is: Make the professors work harder. Humanists today suffer under an increasing demand that their work be economically viable. And that means they must teach more and more courses with greater and greater enrollment. It is unimportant what they teach or who they are; just get cheaper and cheaper instructors to fill the classrooms to bursting. But what will they teach?

The generation of knowledge is as vital to the humanities as it is to every other discipline. Could a scientist today teach the chemistry or biology of 1960? A humanist, however, is assumed to have somehow stored up a lifetime of knowledge in graduate school. Acquiring new knowledge and methods is also part of our job and must be respected. And no scholar can produce knowledge and teach effectively while desperately looking for further part-time teaching.

The humanities are at once the least and the most efficient segment of the university. We don't bring in grants (a fact that today may actually work to our advantage, given the federal government's crackdown on the misuse of grant money), nor do we copyright our products for the benefit of the university (perhaps because of the small return). But we are the repositories of the university's history and future; we do the heavy lifting in teaching the bulk of the students those intellectual skills—critical reading, writing, and thought—that will serve them in any field and any future employment.

Scholars, students, and administrators must all rethink the university. Each generation of intellectuals, from Wilhelm von Humboldt, the creator of the modern research university, to the University of Chicago's great innovator, Robert Maynard Hutchins, also faced this challenge. Were they more successful than we are? They at least recognized that change was needed. Some of us seem still to be driving our father's Oldsmobile and wondering why it does not meet our needs. If the evident crisis of the humanities has any value, it is to make us begin to reconsider the structures and purpose of the university in the post-boom, post–affirmative action, post-expansion, post-book age.

In the end, Chicken Little was right: the sky is falling. But instead of asking how we all can revitalize the humanities, how the humanities can serve an expanded role in the university of the twenty-first century, we attack one another and quibble and weep. Indeed, the December 1997 report of the Modern Language Association on the state of the profession, on which I collaborated, initially received its sharpest critiques from within the profession. Rather than attempt to figure out what they could contribute and place their criticisms as friendly amendments, the critics resorted to hyperbole and blanket attacks, thereby aiding those who aim radically to alter if not to destroy what is clearly the best system of higher education in the world today.

Each setback can be transformed into the possibility for positive change; rotting leaves offer mulch for the flowers of spring. Collapse can lead to new innovations . . . but are we prepared to risk them? Or do we cry, "Ah! It was so good when we were young. Everything was so fine; the world so whole and our youth still intact." No! We must look toward the future and prepare to change. As Rilke said, echoing his own reading of the mad, weeping Nietzsche: You must change your life! *Du muß dein Leben ändern!*

Chapter One

HOW TO GET TENURE

In 1989 I shocked many of my colleagues in departments of German when I published an article titled "Why and How I Study the German" in the *German Quarterly*.[1] I had argued that as teachers of German studies in the United States we should think of ourselves as studying the "Germans" and should develop our own models for doing so. Because of the overwhelmingly strong identification between American German studies and the cultural politics of one or the other of the German states after 1949, North American professors of German were mimicking the questions (and the canon) developed in these states. The result was the isolation of German studies within the American university as professors of German more and more imitated their "German" colleagues and thus had less and less to do with the Anglophone world of North American literary and cultural studies. A great deal of this trend was driven by the ability to raise research money and publish in both Germanys, but primarily in the Federal Republic of Germany.

I received calls and letters from colleagues who said, "Look, I agree with you, but you really shouldn't say this in public" (unspoken was "because you will anger the West Germans who are helping pay for our trips to Germany, our films, our book prizes, our fellowships"). My essay had been the basis of a presentation at a conference held in Philadelphia the year before by the German Academic Exchange Service (DAAD) on the future of German studies. At the meeting I had been even more shocking. I insisted, much to the amusement of the colleagues present, that "where I go, there goes German studies!" This was not at all a narcissistic statement but the obvious (and unrecognized) fact that we—the "certified" members of a profession—at any given time and place determine its structure, direction, and research agenda. This was so in 1973 when I began the first German studies major as chair of the newly reconstituted German studies department at Cornell, and it was true in 1995 in the newly constituted Department of Germanic Studies at the University of Chicago. In 1995, the year that I served as president of the Modern Language Association, an organization of scholars across a wide range of literary and cultural disciplines, I thought it appropriate to imagine the pragmatics of what German studies would mean for the next decade.

The point of departure for these thoughts was an e-mail letter I received from a younger colleague who had taken part in one of my DAAD summer seminars for college teachers a few years earlier. His question was blunt and to the point: What is tenure in German studies, and what do I have to do to get it? He is at a research-oriented institution, so my answer began (like it or not) with the matter of publications. It is, of course, the production of new knowledge in a field that is supposed to set research-oriented institutions of higher learning apart from other institutions.

Yes, other institutions, even if not research-oriented, often stress research, and teaching is important if not vital for tenure at any institution. However, in answering his specific questions I wanted to address the issue of the production and dissemination of knowledge in German studies. What do you teach in the classroom if no new knowledge is being produced? Do you simply recycle your graduate-student notes until they become yellowed with age? And what happens when, as in German studies, the very basis of the field has shifted, when new questions and new approaches have rendered previous approaches and material obsolete?

Attacks on the humanities (such as the label "prof-scam," the accusation that teachers at research institutions were defrauding society by their lack of commitment to teaching and their liberal research agenda) have mocked the role that the humanist, including the teacher of German studies, plays in the production of knowledge. What we do as re-

search is labeled as superficial or trivial or meaningless or—
even worse—politically correct. All these labels attempt to
dismiss basic research in the humanities as not "pragmatic,"
as marginal to the "real" task of higher education: teaching.
Humanists teach, like Socrates; scientists do research, like
Pasteur. (Even Pasteur had better spin doctors in his time
than Socrates did. And Pasteur published; Socrates didn't.
Pasteur was honored; Socrates was poisoned.) Basic research in the sciences fares better today. Few people attack
research in the natural or social sciences even if it has no
obvious "applied" dimension, because we have a collective
hope that such scientific investigations can lead to applied
results in an imagined future.

The research that humanists do also has an applied aspect because it flows directly out of or into our teaching.
Yet the humanist who writes about, say, the German Jewish feminist writer Esther Dischereit, while teaching her
work as a means of understanding the role that literature
has had in post-Wall Germany, or the history of the German novel, or ethnic writing, or the pursuit of an ethical
model in culture, is accused of researching topics that are
too "ivory tower"! ("Ivory tower" today can mean too politically correct.) How should we present our contributions
to scholarship as worthwhile and therefore as a justification
for tenure?

While I was pondering the role of publications in the
tenure process, requests to read the scholarly production of
younger scholars in German studies who were up for promotion, or who intended to apply for competitive fellow-

ships, repeatedly crossed my desk. They too raised the question of what one must do to earn promotion or rewards within the academy. This question is especially important in German studies, where the standards within the field and its very definition have so radically shifted. In the 1960s it was possible to get tenure in German studies (then *Germanistik*) in the United States by editing scholarly texts. My own work in editing collections of sixteenth-century proverbs, as well as the work of the Sturm und Drang writer F. M. Klinger, occupied a large part of my scholarly life. Although I also wrote monographs, textual editing marked my early career. Today this would be impossible in any area of the humanities. The premature closing of the Thomas More edition at Yale is a salient example. The English department there was unwilling to hire anyone to continue it, largely because such scholarship was no longer seen as a rational for academic rewards.

In the fellowship and tenure cases I saw, I could comment only on the projects before me and the publication record of the candidates. I knew little, if anything, about their teaching and service. Certainly there must be clear guidelines, I thought, that I could offer my younger colleague, guidelines that enabled me to evaluate scholarship. I came up with a five-part answer that I now want to share.

1. *Publish in refereed books and journals.* All judgment of scholarship is subjective, but every field has collective norms for judgment. In considering a choice of publishers, ask, Who will read the book for the press? Who will cri-

tique it from the point of view of the wider audience? Who will read it for style and content? Such questions are important, especially for the first-time author. The authority of the specialist in the field provides some context for the new author's work. Ask, too, Will the work be distributed to bookstores, or will it be announced only in a flyer—or not at all? Will your book be merely *printed* or truly *published*?

There is a real difference in North America between vanity publishing and academic publishing, and only some of this distinction has to do with the payment of subventions for publication. Distinguished presses and series may also request subventions, especially in fields with the expectation of limited sales. Certainly there are "famous" cases, such as that of Friedrich Nietzsche, who subvented the publication of many of his own books with very questionable publishers. In Germany it was and is expected that the dissertation and the second thesis be published. Presses have arisen to undertake such tasks, and some of them now have expanded into the North American market. In Germany there are even state sources of support for such publications. Many of these presses function as more antiquated equivalents to the University Microfilm on-demand distribution of dissertations. One can imagine a point in the near future when all theses will be on line (they are now all being written electronically anyway), and we will be able to access each thesis at the university's World Wide Web site, complete with color illustrations and even video clips. There are refereed journals on line now that have made the breakthrough. Yet we continue to publish hard copies of books. Make sure the press is not merely printing but also publishing your book! Publishing is not only making a text available but also vouching for its position in the world of scholarship and making it visible to potential readers.

2. *Publish your work as part of a dialogue in the world of ideas.* All academic books should relate to current scholarly debates. The book can accept these debates and extend them further, or refute them and show how wrong they are in root and branch. Infinite questions can be and have been asked in every field of knowledge. Yet there are always subsets especially important to specific cultures and times. In German studies today, for example, the questions being asked in American German scholarship are much different from those in Germanic scholarship in the new Germany itself. Feminist discourse in American German studies, for example, uses a vocabulary entirely different from that of feminist scholarship in Germany. The very question of the meaning of "gender" is different in Germany. My book *Freud, Race, and Gender* (Princeton University Press, 1993) appeared in Germany as *Freud, Rasse, und Identität.*

Indeed, some questions asked here concern the kinds of problems now being studied in Germany, why these questions are being asked, and how they are being answered. A generation ago (twenty long years), we in North American German studies were asking questions identical to those being asked in West Germany. The cold war was our matrix, and we saw Europe (and Europe saw itself) through certain powerful models. If Alice Kaplan's *French Lessons* is right, this was also true of French studies at the time. We must become aware of the value of our questions and our ability to generate and frame them. Such questions must arise out of our interest and our positionality.

Today the questions and the problems are different, and tomorrow they will be different yet again. It is not that younger scholars must accept ever-changing models in their scholarship, but that our work must respond in one way or another to the concerns of our day. We must not fret that what we do may become outdated, for at some point every question or paradigm will seem passé; nor can we claim any real superiority when our fifteen minutes in the academic limelight occur. All scholarship shifts emphasis over time. At any given moment we need to understand why a specific question, text, or approach resonates in our scholarly community, a community whose perimeters are also always shifting.

3. *Scholarship must present a new or interesting manner of understanding a problem.* Scholarship in the humanities is a big umbrella; it covers all fields and all approaches. Yet there is a fascination in the unknown and the interesting. We search in our scholarship for "truths"—some for truths in our time, others for absolute truths. However, even those who seek absolute truths know that these truths present different facets at different times. Fashion and taste are not supposed to dictate scholarship, yet good scholarship speaks to

the time and its needs. Thus works by great scholars, such as Heinz Politzer's 1966 book *Franz Kafka: Parable and Paradox*, have enduring value; yet, as Mark Anderson has elegantly shown, Politzer avoided the question of the materiality of Kafka's life and world, a materiality that would have included his own body. Anderson's brilliant book *Kafka's Clothes: Ornament and Aestheticism in the Habsburg Fin de Siècle* (1992) alters our understanding of Politzer's Kafka because it asks questions at a very different point in time. Today, in the age of AIDS, questions about meanings ascribed to the body are more important to our understanding of the life and works of an author. We have seen the powerful effect of stigmatizing illnesses, especially those imagined to be sexually transmitted, on the world of culture. The meaning of the Jewish body in the 1960s for a German-Jewish exile poet and critic was quite different and much too close to the bone. Did Politzer's work need to be augmented thirty years after its publication? Of course it did. No scholarship, no matter how great, is ever the final word.

Our own awareness, as scholars, of how our lives and times determine our scholarly questions must be grounded in an understanding of our own roots and desires. Critics in other fields have articulated such positions in a series of brilliant autobiographies. Writers such as Eunice Lipton, Marianna de Marco Torgovnick, Cathy Davidson, Alice Kaplan, and Susan Suleiman reflect on their position as scholars in relation to the world and to their work. Traditionally, scholars have rarely indulged in self-reflection of this sort at the prime of their working lives. Yet these books are not simply the summation of a creative life but rather a contemplation of life events that were important to the scholar and why they shaped her choice of scholarly field and object. In an age of identity politics, studying the "German" as a complex object has meant that all of us—ethnically German or not—have had to ask why we are undertaking this task. In German studies, such self-reflection has rarely taken place for an English-reading audience.[2] Yet it is essential if the critic in German studies is to become aware of the processes within the individual and society by which scholarship becomes important—and to understand that "fashion" in scholarship is a sign of this importance.

4. *Publish for a clearly defined audience.* Whom do you imagine reading your scholarly work (besides your parents)? More and more, I hear from academic publishers that scholars in German studies have stopped buying their books. The assumption is that they have also stopped *reading* scholarly books. The books and essays we produce have to be consumed. Thus a small field, such as German studies, has by definition limited numbers of readers; yet even in the most limited field there have always been writers who can raise the expectations of the reader and the field above the level of minutiae. The works of Andreas Huyssen, Suzanne Zantop, Anton Kaes, Marc Weiner, Eric Santner, and Maria Tatar have reached a wide audience beyond the boundaries of German studies. Others would include the great academic translators in our field, like Krishna Winston, who make complex texts available to the English-

language reading public. Is it possible for this to be at least one of the goals for tenurable scholarship? One hopes so.

5. *Write in an accessible manner.* Every profession has its jargon, the verbal shorthand that makes it possible to communicate complex notions quickly to colleagues working on the same topic. German studies has a number of such idiolects in both German and English. Accessibility of scholarship might be gauged by the use of such language to communicate directly to other specialists concerned with the same problem. Yet truly great scholarship usually has meaning or utility to scholars across a range of fields. The work of relatively few professors of German studies (such as those mentioned above) has been as "useful" to students in postcolonial studies, English, children's literature, French literature, and intellectual history as to those in German studies. First-rate scholarship should provide a model for approaching a topic as well as solid and substantial content. Such scholarship is usually especially accessible. Elaine Showalter recently insisted to me that scholarly books must be readable books. This quality should be a requirement for first-rate scholarship.

The language of such scholarship is not incidental. While it is possible that scholars in the Anglophone critical world might seek to address German colleagues on topics of common interest in German, at least at present such occasions are relatively infrequent. Our critical world should be the world of the Anglophone humanist whose work is of interest and use to scholars and teachers in other fields within our critical universe. It is possible that there are moments of convergence in certain arenas, but the aim should be to speak across the departmental borders at our institutions, even if the objects are canonical. Part of the motivation is self-defense: if we speak only to colleagues in Germany, and speak to them in German, we lose the potential for dialogue with our neighbors. But part of it is the sense that we have more in common—the study of the language, literature, and culture of a non-Anglophone world—with those who study French, Italian, and Japanese literature and culture than with the object of study itself.

From Kuno Francke, the professor of German at Harvard (and a paid agent of the Kaiser) at the turn of the century to the political and economic refugees of the 1930s through the 1960s, great Germanic scholarship was undertaken in the United States. In those years the interests of American and German scholars overlapped more substantially. German studies was defined by the Germans, and the dialogue was among "Germans" in whatever nation (and of whatever nationality and language) they found themselves. This created an illusion of "international *Germanistik*" that was, of course, rooted in the interests, desires, and financing of the German government. It was (and is) cultural propaganda of the first order. German departments wrote and taught in German for other scholars who wrote and taught in German. The pragmatic result was the linguistic and critical isolation of German departments, which became German-speaking islands in an English-speaking world.

While they could have entered into dialogue with the broader field, they didn't.

Quite the opposite is now the case. The very model of German studies that brings together all of those working on the object "Germany" (however defined) means that such scholarship must be accessible across disciplinary rather than geographic boundaries. And yet in these departments the language and its relationship to the culture remain paramount. We must be able to "code-shift," moving elegantly between a command of the language and culture of our object of study and an awareness of the purpose of that research for the culture in which we live, learn, and teach.

My hope for the next ten years is that many more books and articles of this "ideal" type will cross my desk and be read by colleagues in many fields besides our own. We have begun to think about the study of the "German" as a field as complex and fraught with difficulties as, say, American studies—not bad for twenty years of change.

Chapter Two

TEACHING AND

RESEARCHING

IN THE

HUMANITIES

FROM A

TRANSDISCIPLINARY

PERSPECTIVE

When I stand before a classroom full of undergraduates or sit in a seminar with graduate students, the common assumption is that I—as a teacher and scholar—will present some corner of the knowledge in my field. I am an expert, and, to the best of my ability, my job should be to illuminate the unknowing about my subject matter.

But where does the knowledge come from? Is it simply the product of historical accretion—the accumulation of the knowledge and questions of the past—or do I, the expert, help shape, change, and focus it? The Straussian assumption that knowledge is "found," that it is passed down uninterpreted from great thinkers of the past, has reappeared in recent attacks on the North American university. "We must return to the canon of texts that form the absolute basis of Western Knowledge!" shout critics, from the philosopher Allan Bloom to the former director of the National Endowment for the Humanities, Lynne Cheney. "Teachers are spending too much time doing needless, pointless scholarship!" they cry. "What they should be doing is teaching—and the more students the better!" resounds the solution. This cry for "productivity" is echoed in the administrative halls of many universities.

Now, those of us who know anything about the history of the modern university know that myths about the permanence of values in scholarship, and its relationship to teaching, were developed during the early nineteenth century, exactly when the modern research university was being created. Between 1800 and 1900 the definition of knowledge, in the humanities as in the sciences, was undergoing radical change. Academic disciplines as we now know them were being created: physics and psychology stopped being part of departments of philosophy, and new texts (such as Shakespeare and Goethe) were being added to the university curriculum.

During the nineteenth century there was a vast shift in what was to be taught and how it was to be presented. The final secularization of the university demanded entirely new models of interpretation and investigation and the establishment of completely new fields. Some of these did not survive (such as phrenology at the University of Edinburgh), but many did. From classical philology to the study of modern vernacular literature, what was to be taught in the humanities, as much as in any other arena of knowledge, was the subject of harsh, acrimonious exchange. When the classical philologist Friedrich Nietzsche, the youngest individual ever to hold a chair in the Swiss university system, opened his course of public lectures in Zurich in the 1870s with a talk on the nature of the university and its rationale, he was disparaged by his older contemporaries, who dismissed him as a "tenured radical."

In the United States and Europe during the same period, the rise of the natural sciences, both theoretical and applied, established a model in which the university's role in "pure research" (earlier limited to the scientific academies) was as important as its "teaching." By the end of the nineteenth century the universities had become centers for research and teaching in the natural sciences as well as in the humanities. Central to this model was the belief that knowledge was present in the universe and only needed to be uncovered. This process of "uncovering" was undertaken through human agency, but it was independent of the vagaries of human difference and individual bias. By the close of the nineteenth century, positivism defined the role of the investigator as well as the teacher.

In no other field in the humanities was this more evident than in the invention of German studies by early nineteenth-century German scholars such as Wilhelm and Jacob Grimm. Up to that point German studies simply did not exist. With the construction of a fabled German identity—in the absence of a German state—German studies came to be the place where German political culture, as a source of political identity, was defined. It was defined not primarily in terms of literary culture but in the history of law, the history of the German language, and the history of popular literary forms, such as the fairy tale and the proverb (in the work of K. F. W. Wander). This work was highly ideologically motivated, as we have learned from the work of scholars such as John Ellis and Maria Tatar, but motivated from the left. The political trajectory of the Brothers Grimm and their colleagues was revolutionary, or at least "liberal."

This revolution in knowledge placed the study of German culture at the center of a new "science of humanities," as it came to be called. These scholars were self-consciously involved in redefining both German and European ideas of the boundaries of knowledge. They had their intellectual precursors: the enlightened Protestant theologian Johann Gottfried Herder had explored the meaning and structure of popular German poetry, along with Homer and the Bible, at the close of the eighteenth century. The restructuring of the role of the Germans in Western culture was part of the inheritance of the European Enlightenment. Nineteenth-century scholarship claimed, however, that the study of the "science of humanities" was a neutral, distanced investigation. Studies of the literature of the "golden age of German culture," for example, undertaken within this tradition, provided a reading of the historical "facts" about the rise of German middle-class culture in the late Middle Ages. However, they also provided an idealized model for the sort of cultural integration desired and represented by the liberal scholars writing in mid-nineteenth-century Germany.

German literary scholarship (*Germanistik*), as Peter Hohendahl has shown,[1] fled further and further into an aestheticized sense of the inherent uniqueness of the literary object. This became evident as literary history came to define itself as separate and distinct from (and perhaps better than) all other forms of history. The abandonment of such a view—without trashing the objects of literary history—has meant that the literary text has become more and more important to German studies. No longer is it either a "beautiful world" into which to flee the realities of daily life or a source of facts about a specific period in history. Historians, literary critics, cultural studies specialists, and political scientists (at least those in the fuzzy area of political philosophy and political psychology) are now using texts as a way of exploring the fantasies of a culture or an epoch. Here the traditional tools of literary exegesis, of how to read a complex text, have become a vital component of many fields within German studies.

In the post-Shoah world, German studies stands at a new crossroads in the development of the science of humanities. German studies now embraces everything from the medieval and early modern world to the culture, politics, and history of contemporary Germany. Indeed, even the study of the marginal German literatures, such as the literature of German colonialism or of the German communities in Bohemia and Romania, so radically rejected by the nineteenth-century originators of German studies and later so compromised by their Nazi advocates, now represents a new field of scrutiny. The study of the new multicultural society of the Berlin Republic, its literature and cinema, flourishes within the new German studies. This discipline, originally created to span the traditional divisions of scholarship and knowledge (the academic departments), has opened itself up to true innovations in scholarship within the past decade. The study of the meaning of the literary text—with its deconstructive, poststructuralist, and postcolonial models—has been applied with extraordinary results to the traditional canon, from Wolfram von Eschenbach to Christa Wolf and beyond. The impact of the Shoah and Jewish studies on German studies has been wide-ranging. With the shifts of population in Europe, the problem of assimilation in a society that desired homogeneity—once considered the "Jewish problem"—is now being experienced (and written about) by writers and essayists of Turkish, Asian, and African background or origin. (Indeed, one of the central problems experienced by Jewish writers in the post-unification climate is whether they belong to the general culture, which wants to assimilate them as a sign of its liberality, or are marginal to this culture, in ways analogous to other minority writers.) The very concept of regional studies—once so neatly defined by the Iron Curtain and the Department of Education, which funded "Western" or "Eastern" centers and projects —has become muddled in the past few years. Does German culture in Russia or Poland again count as Western

European culture? Does Yiddish again count as an Eastern European language? What will European economic unification and expansion do to the fantasies about a reunited Germany? What texts will be central to German Studies in the future? New texts and new problems cross department boundaries as historians, anthropologists, and sociologists discover the textual tradition at the center of traditional *Germanistik*, and literary and cultural scholars explore the theoretical models provided by wider-ranging theories in which texts hold a central importance. My own research in the reappearance of Jewish writing in Germany—some of it in English, such as the work of Irene Dische and Susan Neiman—reveals a finely drawn web that permits the examination and reconstruction of what the German is today thought to be, and not to be. The recent work of some German American scholars, as I discuss in Chapter 7, has pointed to the importance of a parallel tradition: the existence in nineteenth-century American culture of a vibrant German-language literary tradition. In such a case even the question of language as the prime indicator of cultural tradition can be drawn into question.

Anthropologists and historians of anthropology have suddenly become more important in German studies as interest grows in understanding the meaning of, and the meaning ascribed to, German ritual practices, from dueling fraternities to Wild West clubs. Feminist scholars (both women and men) have raised questions about the meaning and representation of the feminine in German culture and thought. All of these approaches are fruitful because they provide the basic knowledge for us to ask the questions relevant to our own time. They provide tools for reexamining the past (yes, even our own past) and for exploring how and why we ask the questions that seem important to us. In all of these fields, scholars of German ancestry in the United States are increasingly laboring alongside non-German scholars (among them, minorities).

These changes give rise to the same sorts of tensions within German studies as within other areas of humanist scholarship. My personal expertise is only as good as the new questions I can evolve to provide new information and approaches to both traditional and innovative areas of study. Like the extraordinary scholars of the nineteenth century who created German studies, scholars today confront the traditional attitude that we already know enough, we have enough unanswered questions, we have done enough work. (The field is sufficiently well defined for everybody to carve out a piece of territory and relax!) The response is that no body of knowledge is fixed, and that the very asking of questions across the bounds of traditional knowledge provides answers (and questions) for each age. Our questions reveal as much about our sense of historical location as the questions asked (and answered) by the creators of German studies almost a hundred years ago reveal about them.

Teaching and research; research and teaching—these involve asking new questions, creating new disciplines, restructuring older fields, exploring and experimenting. Nevertheless, all along, the myth has been maintained that this knowledge (and its means of presentation) was simply to be found in nature. As with Michelangelo's claim that he merely uncovered the beautiful sculpture enclosed within the block of marble, the academic has argued that the uncovering of knowledge was simply a natural act, a revealing of that which was present. Teaching too was seen as natural: it was the continuation of ancient established models of transferring the information thus uncovered. In the nineteenth century, during the establishment of the university as we know it, with its seemingly universal set of disciplines, the origin invoked for the method of teaching was usually ancient Greece—an ancient Greece, of course, carefully constructed by nineteenth-century thinkers such as Matthew Arnold to justify their own claims for the permanence of their new, radical, and loudly opposed innovations in teaching.

At the end of the twentieth century we have so enshrined the notion of the permanence of knowledge that we need to ask: What knowledge is taught in the classroom, and where does it come from? My own approach has been both discipline-based and also transdisciplinary. Assuming that the division of knowledge is not the reflex of some natural law, I argue that restructuring disciplines and rethinking their goals is a natural and regular procedure in the university, and that the claim to universality or permanence of established or even innovative approaches to teaching and research is an equal part of this constant, dynamic drive for new knowledge and its dissemination.

In the natural sciences and in the related professions

such as medicine, the boundaries of the disciplines shift and teaching approaches change over relatively short stretches of time. The neat divisions between chemistry and biology that were in place when I was an undergraduate in the 1960s have simply vanished: introductory courses in physiology spend almost as much time on human biochemistry as they do on gross anatomy.

The revolutionary shifts in the acceptance of scientific innovation—well studied by the historians and sociologists of science—show how a gradual accumulation of knowledge can shift, create, or dismantle an entire discipline, often within a generation. After a generation, few if any scientists subscribe to the older model. In the humanities, the ability to argue that any change is evil has altered our attitudes toward knowledge. The late-nineteenth-century model, which held that the sciences understand by acquiring new knowledge and the humanities by incrementally hoarding old knowledge, did not reflect even the realities of the German university out of which it came. The "revolutionary" model of science has been viewed as the "natural" progression of science. Built into this shift is a resistance by those invested in the older models of science, and thus one needs to speak of "revolutions" in scientific thought. To teach the science of the past unchanged and to teach it in the same way one was taught it is unacceptable once a scientific revolution takes place. And no evocation of the "great tradition" and the "important figures" and the "centrality of a specific approach" will rescue old science. As Enrico Fermi is said to have observed when he saw undergraduates in the

1940s reading Isaac Newton's paper on gravity in the core science course: "That's nice, but it's not physics."

But what about the humanities? Here we have recently (and loudly) heard the laments for the abandonment of the center of the humanities, of the basic values of Western society. Why, these impassioned critics ask, are humanists not content with the knowledge, the texts, the approaches handed down from the now-mythic Greece of Aristotle, the Oxbridge of Cardinal Newman, or the University of Chicago of Leo Strauss? At the end of the twentieth century there was an explosion of new ways of thinking about the humanities; new paths were cut across the existing divisions of knowledge. Opposition to these developments came from professors who knew what the divisions of knowledge had to be—because they created them, or were trained in them and employed to teach them. That these divisions no longer were seen as absolute, and that new absolutes were being generated to replace them, caused a reappearance of precisely the same conflicts that have always appeared.

In the humanities, the question, What do I teach? has become important again. The loosening of the boundaries between the traditional fields of knowledge (from history to English, from anthropology to religion) has given rise to questions that are not easily accommodated within these older divisions of knowledge. Nevertheless, these categories themselves are historically limited; some of them are very new to the university. (The first chair in English, for example, was established not much more than a hundred years ago.) Transdisciplinary studies stands—at this point—above existing disciplinary lines and is generating the sort of questions that link, but also may transcend, existing disciplines. Are questions about identity and identity formation in a cultural setting, for example, to be answered by departments of history, English, psychology, or religion? Or do all of these divisions of knowledge contain objects and approaches that may be of use in exploring how we become who we are—and how individuals in other times and cultures became who they were, and how they recorded this development? My own work on stereotyping and its representation within cultural artifacts, ranging from literary texts to medical monographs, rests on work done by scholars in a number of existing disciplines but also (I hope) contributes questions to be asked from both within and outside such disciplines. Newly established fields, such as gender studies, by definition cut across the boundaries of existing fields, even those (such as sociology or literature) where relevant questions are being pursued. Such fields can approach the transdisciplinary, can raise questions and approaches to teaching that are of interest to scholars in many fields and that also may turn (or may have turned) themselves into disciplines, with their own approaches and codes of knowledge.

These transformations mean that each humanist can play a major role in generating knowledge. Moreover, if one is lucky, this knowledge will become part of what is taught. That is one of the rubs. When one assumes that there is a permanent stock of knowledge with permanent, immutable borders and an established manner of teaching it, some humanists will indeed teach exactly what they learned in graduate school and, captivated by the illusion of the immutability of knowledge, will never question the premises of what they know. Whereas in the sciences such attitudes lead to regular "revolutions"—the overthrow of accepted, permanent systems of thought—in the humanities the permanence of knowledge is assumed.

There are also humanists of many stripes who pursue questions and present solutions that reveal themselves not to be useful additions to the stock of knowledge for the present. Whether they may have importance in the future is an unanswerable question. Do we censor these scholars and encourage only those whose work seems useful to us? Do we censor the scholars who are "abandoning" the traditions and striving for innovation? The tradition within the liberal arts sadly has been a pragmatic one. We reward the models of scholarship that "we" (the consensus of the university) deem to be important. We reward them with tenure and grants and prestige. However, the other paths too must have a place in the pursuit of knowledge and the ability to present that knowledge before peers and students alike.

We see today fissures that are the healthy sign of a dynamic, living search for knowledge in the humanities; a search for knowledge that, in spite of myths about the permanence and immutability of humanistic truths, has always been the practice in the humanities. This new knowledge has always been sought in the interstices between existing disciplines; these boundary areas often then become the new divisions of labor, which will again serve to preserve knowledge, and against which new forces will have to labor. Research in the humanities, even the most abstract and basic research, fuels these changes. When the humanist enters the classroom, it must be with a sense of involvement in the continuing generation of knowledge and the experimentation in how this knowledge is to be presented. Otherwise, what is taught are the revolutionary lessons of the past—entombed, desiccated, and reduced to unquestioned truths.

Chapter Three

SOME MODELS OF

INTERDISCIPLINARY

TEACHING

When I was a graduate student at Tulane University in the 1960s, I was "taught" how to teach language. That is, I was given a script and told exactly what to do each day, without any deviations. I was a human adjunct to the newest technology of the sixties, the language laboratory, with its spinning, synchronized tape recorders and spaceship-like monitoring station. I was to drill students, not teach them. My job was to be as precise as the machines were. My graduate seminars, by contrast, had always been Socratic in form. In them I intuitively learned more about teaching: always know more than the students, ask them questions to which you alone know the true answer, be the authority in the classroom.

The shock came with my first real job teaching at St. Mary's Dominican College, a Catholic women's college in New Orleans. There was no machinery to fall back on in the language classes. In the literature class, I felt a true panic that I really didn't know more than the students did. Over the past thirty years, class by class, seminar by seminar, I have slowly learned how to teach. I have adapted the Socratic method so that I actually ask questions to which I don't know the "right" answers. (This is very unnerving for students who take notes in order to have the right answer on the examination.) I have learned to lecture to large groups of students in such a way as not (immediately) to put them to sleep. (Some undergraduates seem to sleep everywhere but in their dormitories at night.) I learned to see technology of all types—from computers to video—not as a master but as a potential ally. Slowly I realized that teaching meant constantly learning new means of communicating the research that I was doing outside the classroom to very different types of students in the classroom. The classroom came to be my laboratory, where I tested my ideas (and those of others) against the combined insight and intelligence of my students—and the students often won. But every group of students demanded new and different styles of teaching.

After a dozen years of teaching, I was confronted with a new challenge. In the 1970s I was asked by the dean of the Cornell Medical College to develop a medical humanities course. The idea was that introducing the humanities and ethics into the professional schools would make students more humane and more ethical. We learned quickly that exposure to ideas does not change values or attitudes.

In my first year at the medical college, I fell into the error of lecturing to the medical students. They slept as soundly as many of my undergraduates. Before the second year began I was desperate. I turned to my friend Larry Palmer, a professor of law at Cornell. He suggested that I visit the law school and observe the use of the case method and role-playing in teaching law. I was impressed because it was virtually impossible for students to be passive in such an environment. When students did not know when they would be asked to participate, when they had to study a case in all of its aspects and think out each of the implications, being passive was out of the question.

I adapted the case method for the medical school. I created scenarios, some taken from real-life cases, some invented, some based on literary models, in which the roles were prepared by the students. We read legal cases from the history of modern medicine, such as the "Jewish Chronic Disease Hospital Case" of the 1950s concerning a patient's need to give informed consent for treatment. We read literary cases, such as Henrik Ibsen's *Enemy of the People*, examining the obligations of the physician toward the health of the public, or short stories by Richard Selzer on surgery. The students were assigned roles that they had to prepare. The student assigned to be a surgical nurse in a case would have to interview a surgical nurse and base the role on that information. Constructing their roles from readings and interviews, the students had to be consistent in their representing the views, and they had to be able to argue from the point of view of their roles. If we covered a legal case, they had to understand the position of the protagonists; if a literary text, they had to extrapolate a position from the plot and character of the figures in the dramas. The goal was to show how individuals' choices were determined by their position, in history, society, and the structures of medicine. Suddenly, medical humanities came to be a place where one was able to ask very hard questions about "what would I have done," rather than come up with idealized scenarios that ignore the complexities of the time and place of every choice.

Was the course a success? Well, 25 percent of the students hated it. They felt that it was a waste of time; it had nothing to do with "real" medicine, which they defined as "science." Twenty-five percent of the students loved the course and saw it as central in helping them understand their roles as physicians and the historical and cultural specificity of the medical world. Fifty percent were neutral, but because everyone had to take roles during the semester, and because everyone got to ask questions of the role players each time, no one slept!

Each course I teach is different from the last. Sometimes it is radically different in form and content; sometimes it is marginally different simply because of the nature of the specific group of students. And yet the nuances of difference make teaching exciting, especially interdisciplinary teaching. Teaching undergraduates can be just as challenging as teaching graduate or professional students. Since the early 1970s I have regularly taught an introduction to psychoanalytic theory for undergraduates at Cornell University and the University of Chicago. This course is usually listed in the departments of comparative literature, German studies, English, and psychology. The enrollment runs from approximately 60 to, most recently, more than 250 undergraduates (and some graduates). The purpose of the course is straightforward. Given that many of my colleagues in the humanities (and some in the social sciences) use psychoanalytic models of one sort or another in their teaching and scholarship, it seemed to me necessary to offer an introductory course on psychoanalysis that would enable students both to read Freud's texts in a historical context and to follow the development of psychoanalysis as theory, therapy, and model of critical analysis since Freud. For someone like myself, from a German department, it was also a chance to show how the study of a major cultural figure and his theory contributes to a general university education.

The requirements for the course have always included a writing assignment. Students are offered a range of topics, ranging from the application of psychoanalytic models discussed in class to texts (literary or cultural) of their own choosing to a paper on psychoanalytic theory or the option of keeping a "dream diary" and presenting an analysis of one of the dreams recorded. (This mode of teaching was pioneered by Jeffrey Berman of the State University of

New York at Albany.) For the latter, complete confidentiality is guaranteed the student; only I will read and comment on the dream and its interpretation. To prepare for the latter, the students read Freud's summary essay "On Dreams" and the chapter from *The Interpretation of Dreams* on the "specimen dream," the dream of Irma's injection. They also hear a detailed lecture on the debates about dreams and dreaming following Freud, both within psychoanalytic theory and in the medical literature on sleep.

Here I present one dream and analysis in detail and compare the presentation with analogous cases from the class material. I have masked the dream material and have combined material from a number of classes so as to make identification of individuals impossible. My purpose in this essay is to examine the advantages to the use of the dream diary and dream analysis for undergraduate instruction rather than to explore the themes developed in this material. The student in this example is a male, sophomore, with a proposed major in psychology. He comes from a large urban area and is one of three siblings.

THE AIRPORT DREAM, MARCH 20–21, 19XX

I am talking to my sister on the telephone under the pretext that it is my responsibility to pick her up from the airport. I tell her that I'm not sure where I should pick her up, and I give her these vague instructions: "You should ask someone when you arrive there." She scolds me, "It's your responsibility to find out, so find out."

Next, I am in the airport, standing in a supermarket checkout line, reading a newspaper. I look around nervously. I move my possessions (a carry-on and a camera case) over the bar decoder, and I move myself through the checkout aisle. The checkout woman, whom I recognize as Jane Pauley, the TV news personality, asks me why I've chosen to take the controversial photograph of a girl scout in a torn dress. I reply, "Let's take a look at it." I spread out my newspaper on the floor, and we bend down to look at the photograph, which has been published in the newspaper. The photograph is of a young girl (eight to ten years old) with blond hair. She wears a torn dress, and her face is dirty.

I become extremely self-conscious. After stumbling over words, I say, "I'm trying to show the socioeconomic plight of the girl scout." This explanation rings false to me. The Jane Pauley figure chastises me: "As a photojournalist, you must learn to be straightforward."

Next, I am standing in front of a large airport window, watching the planes land and hoping to find my sister. I suddenly realize that I'm no longer holding my possessions. I have a premonition that my camera is being stolen. I frantically turn around, and I see that a shadowy man dressed in dirty rags is standing over my belongings. I can only see him from behind. He bends down in slow motion, preparing to grab the camera. As I run to him, he grabs my camera. I jump on his back. I can hear people laugh as I wrestle him to the floor. I contemplate shooting him, and the dream ends in an unidentified gunshot.

THE STUDENT'S ANALYSIS

I am talking to my sister on the telephone under the pretext that it is my responsibility to pick her up from the airport. • It corresponds with an event of the previous day, which has set the dream in motion (cf. Sigmund Freud, *The Interpretation of Dreams* [New York: Avon Books, 1965], 197). During a telephone conversation with my sister Karen, we discussed her upcoming visit to Cornell. Although she was planning to travel by car, the airport scenario was fresh in mind from my recent travels via airplane to see another sister, Jacqueline. (The work of condensation.)

I tell her that I'm not sure where I should pick her up, and I give her these vague instructions: "You should ask someone when you arrive there." She scolds me, "It's your responsibility to find out, so find out." • A similar exchange occurred in the reallife phone conversation. Karen asked me to find out about the parking and weather situations. I replied, "I will try, but I'm very busy. You can look in *USA Today* for the weather, and for parking, ask the workers in the street booths when you arrive." Karen reacted vehemently to my vague and lazy instructions; she became the authoritarian older sister that I disfavor. It was a chaotic week for me, and I was finding it difficult to keep a rein on the gridlock of competing elements in my life. So in the dream, "You should ask someone when you arrive there" was my liberation tactic, an escapist answer to the external conditions which vie for my attention.

I am in the airport, standing in a supermarket checkout line,

reading a newspaper. I look around nervously. I move my posses-
sions (a carry-on and a camera case) over the bar decoder, and I
move myself through the checkout aisle. • I had recently taken
my first trip to Wegman's and was struck by the conven-
ience of their checkout system. So, in one respect, the in-
clusion of the supermarket checkout line in the dream represents my desire to impose order on my life. It is an
example of the "displacement" of dream work: an important dream thought and indifferent dream picture (checkout line) dramatize order. It is at this point in the dream
that my anxiety begins to take shape: "I look around nervously." Suddenly, I am the one taking the trip. According to
Freud, "'Departing' on a journey is one of the commonest
and best authenticated symbols of death" (420). More re-
vealingly, "Luggage that one travels with is a load of sin . . .
that weighs one down" (393). The fact that I push my "load
of sin" over the bar decoder is significant. I am "pricing"
my sins, perhaps an unconscious appeal to the conscious
attitude to weigh the significance of my actions. On the
other hand, I also push my camera over the decoder. To
me, my camera represents the way I see the world. The
camera may be a displaced representation of my value system. However, I had recently fought with my girlfriend
about some nude photographs which I had taken. I ended
up feeling guilty about the photographs. Thus, my camera
also belongs with the "load of sin." I associate the "newspaper" with my earlier reference to *USA Today* (I had
asked Karen to research that newspaper's weather report)
and with the guilty feelings which arose from that request.

Here, we see the first connections of guilt and sexuality in the dream, for my action of moving through the checkout aisle connotes sexual intercourse (422).

The checkout woman, whom I recognize as Jane Pauley, the TV news personality, asks me why I've chosen to take the controversial photograph of a girl scout in a torn dress. I reply, "Let's take a look at it." I spread out my newspaper on the floor, and we bend down to look at the photograph, which has been published in the newspaper. The photograph is of a young girl (eight to ten years old) with blond hair. She wears a torn dress, and her face is dirty. • I had recently read an article (in a newspaper) about an AIDS special that Jane Pauley was hosting. Therefore, her presence in the dream underscores the theme of my sexual anxiety. The "girl scout in a torn dress" stirs a memory from my recent trip to see Jacqueline. During my stay at Jacqueline's house in Colorado, I met the nine-year-old daughter of her roommate. The precocious girl was talkative. She recounted her recent girl scout camping trip for me, and spoke gleefully about how dirty she had become. At the time of her storytelling, I had just come back from a photography expedition. I contemplated whether or not I should take her picture. I did not. She had long blond hair like the girl in the dream photograph.

I become extremely self-conscious. After stumbling over words, I say, "I'm trying to show the socioeconomic plight of the girl scout." This explanation rings false to me. • This is the point in the dream interpretation where I've had to suppress my critical faculty the most (134). I had tried to dismiss the significance of the young girl in my dream, but I've realized that she is the fulcrum of its pathology. I felt a strong sexual attraction to her. In fact, I felt a strange self-consciousness when I was around her, just as I did in the dream. But the dream's self-consciousness stems from my fear that my desires will be revealed by the newswoman. Thus my feigned concern for "the socioeconomic plight of the girl scout": I am covering up my real motives for "taking the photograph" by hiding behind the façade of philanthropy.

The Jane Pauley figure chastises me: "As a photojournalist, you must learn to be straightforward." • In waking life, I am a photojournalist for a local newspaper. It had been a bad week at work. I had a disagreement with my boss over one of my photographs. He felt that the photograph was too subjective. I have a strong aversion to authority figures, often, I fear, because they are in positions to reveal that I am, in some way, a fraud. This is the second dream instance in which I am being told what to do by an authority figure (the work of condensation). Karen's orders in the beginning of the dream, "It's your responsibility," also stemmed from my inability to give "straightforward" instructions. So, as I interpret, I search for what is crooked.

I suddenly realize that I'm no longer holding my possessions. I have a premonition that my camera is being stolen. I frantically turn around, and I see that a shadowy man dressed in dirty rags is standing over my belongings. I can only see him from behind. He bends down in slow motion, preparing to grab the camera. • By neglecting my baggage, I have attempted to leave behind the "sins" that weigh me down. In the dream, it doesn't faze me that I've left my carry-on of "sins" behind, but I am struck with terror when I realize that I've neglected the camera—my value system. I discover that "a shadowy man dressed in dirty rags" is threatening to steal my value system. This semester I've been studying Jungian psychology. When the dream occurred, I had been reading about "the shadow archetype." It seems to me that this "shadowy man" is a figure from shadow psychology. He represents "the dangerous aspect of the unrecognized dark half of [my] personality" (C. J. Jung, *Two Essays on Analytical Psychology* [New York: Bollingen Foundation, Inc., 1953], 96). In the dream he is "unrecognized," for "I can only see him from behind." Who exactly is this shadow with the "dirty rags"? Freud provides me with an important clue when he equates uncleanness with avarice in dream interpretation (233). This equation has forced me to scrutinize my own avaricious actions. Just as the "shadowy man" attempts to steal my camera (and value system), I recently neglected my own value system by taking a liberal amount of photographic material from the newspaper headquarters. Now, Jane Pauley's reproof—"As a photojournalist, you must learn to be straightforward"— takes on a new meaning: "On the job, you must learn to be honest." I can also now interpret the meaning behind the "dirty" face of the young girl in the dream photograph. In my fantasies, I was *stealing* away the innocence of the young girl. By projecting my avariciousness onto the face I so admired, I could gain immunity. My guilt was only to be revealed by my self-consciousness. (One further, disconnected thought about the young girl: Freud writes that he has "come across undoubted cases in which sisters symbolize breasts" [393]. Just as my sister does not arrive in the dream, neither have the breasts of the girl scout, a fact that I observed in waking life.)

As I run to him, he grabs my camera. I jump on his back. I can hear people laugh as I wrestle him to the floor. I contemplate shooting him, and the dream ends in an unidentified gunshot. • My ego confronts its shadow and struggles with it. I am trying to dominate the dark aspects of my personality. The laughter symbolizes the insecurities that arise from the shadow conflict. I hypothesize that the "unidentified gunshot" came from external sensory stimuli (56). My dorm room is adjacent to a bathroom where toilet seats are carelessly dropped. The "gunshot" bang wakes me up often.

My "Airport Dream" may be what Freud calls a "punishment dream." "What is fulfilled in them is equally an unconscious wish, namely a wish that the dreamer may be punished for a repressed and forbidden wishful impulse" (596). Two forbidden wishful impulses are clearly represented in my dream: the wish to steal, and the wish to *take the photograph* of young girls. These are the latent thoughts that have produced the psychical energy for my dream's construction. Freud says that "the repressed wish comes out in the form of anxiety" (621). Anxiety pervades the "Airport Dream," namely in my fear of being revealed. As a result of the "condensation" of dream work, my fear of being revealed is represented by several images; i.e., by Jane Pauley and the bar decoder and the laughter (Sigmund Freud, *New Introductory Lectures on Psychoanalysis* [New York: W. W.

Norton and Company, Inc., 1965], 20). To borrow Freud's words, "Humiliating thoughts that poured cold water on the fantasy found their way into the dream" (513). The dream may also be a pure wish-fulfillment dream in which my sense of morality learns to recognize its opposite; I confront the "private life," the shadow, behind the mask of values. The dream's early emphasis on my preoccupation with order represents this active attempt of my unconscious to resolve the tension of opposites, as does my struggle with the shadowy man at the dream's end. I have difficulty finding clear-cut allusions to scenes from my childhood in this dream. However, I would speculate that my crush on the young girl is the product of unfulfilled crushes from my childhood. I can remember painful rejections from girls that I "loved" in elementary school. Perhaps these distressing events contributed some energy for the dream.

The dream and its interpretation, as with most of these student analyses, remain fixated at the level of day-residue and sexual analogies in the day-residue. Another male student writes of a dream that came following "a long and very painful break-up with my girlfriend of three years," a factor that plays no overt role in either the dream narrated or in his analysis. The awareness of day-residue as the primary focus of these analyses is striking. It reveals a deep-seated focus on the "real" and the "experienced." For the core of these dream analyses is the anxiety about fantasy, unless it can be anchored in some type of experiential frame. Thus, another student, a female undergraduate, provides a long (and insightful) analysis of the day-residue in a dream that centers on a classroom situation in which a lost paper and this class itself appeared. The analysis of the dream moves elegantly back into early childhood, but the thrust of the childhood analysis reflects a real "traumatic childhood experience," a near-accident experienced by her mother when the student was five years old. The key to dream analysis for undergraduates in a classroom is the reflection of a reality. The role of fantasy and personality development is lacking, except as a means of reading the "symbolic" into the classroom situation.

The question of the retreat to the real in the narration of dream events by eighteen- to twenty-two-year-olds is central to any analysis of the use of dream diaries in a classroom situation. Students of this age group unexposed to actual analytic practice focus not on the symbolic but rather on the real. This flight into the real often masks the more difficult and complex questions that surface. The relationship with parents or siblings is read through "adult" experience. Childhood memories, if evoked at all, tend to be read as real prefigurations of later conflicts or as mere day-residue. Questions of the subjectivity of the dreamers and their ambiguous relationship to their not quite completely formed superegos are almost always repressed. Images of the internalized parent, which are often overtly projected onto or into the "real" memories that are seen to make up the substance of the dream, are masked or repressed.

These exercises are valuable. Students learn to remember their dreams. If used appropriately in the classroom, they nurture the student's awareness of the constructedness of his or her own sense of self, as mirrored in the dream state. More important, they provide the needed empirical evidence of "real" dreams for the student. One of the problems raised in the debates about the status of psychoanalysis is its scientific status, however that is defined, and undergraduates develop a sense of what "real" science is from their exposure to our culture. Here the experience of learning to record dreams becomes as strongly empirical an experience as the work in the chemistry or genetics laboratory. What these students do with their dreams is, however, bounded by the same ideology. They need to understand the dream as a mimetic or even symbolic reflection of their actual, recalled daily experience.

The role of the dream diary in the classroom is thus at least twofold. It provides an exercise that replicates the Freudian experience of self-analysis; it provides a means of applying dream analysis; and it provides a "scientific" basis for the study of psychoanalysis. All three factors contribute to a high level of student satisfaction with these exercises. Indeed, students who choose to do a dream diary and analysis regularly rate the written exercises in the course more highly than those who opt for a more traditional term paper. The instructor must remember that this is not a "real" dream analysis and keep its limitations in mind when the exercise is read; yet the analyses must still be treated with all of the care and concern for privacy that would be part of any analytic exchange.

Such innovative approaches are the sort of models that

we must constantly evolve if we are to be effective teachers of the humanities. The role of such innovative teaching within traditional literature, language, and cultural departments in no way violates the disciplinary presumptions of these fields. Freudian psychoanalysis was a product of Viennese scientific culture. The original texts are in German (and some students are inspired to learn the language in order to read them). The means of providing students access to the ideas and implications of such texts and their underlying cultural implications can be as varied and complex as the texts themselves. The "sample" dream diary is intended to encourage teachers of German studies who have interest and expertise in such areas central to the discipline to apply broader (and indeed riskier) techniques in the classroom. This does not turn the classroom into a group analysis session but applies the ideas and methodologies learned in the classroom to a "real" situation—the examination of the internal life of the student using the paradigm of Freudian psychoanalysis.

Chapter Four

HABENT SUA

FATA LIBELLI

Books, Jobs,

and the MLA

Terence remarked that books have their fates. Many are one day in fashion, the next discarded. The remainder tables at Barnes and Noble or Powell's reflect last week's or last month's reading. These books—our books—have their fate; but so do their authors and their readers. Here I want to speak of that double fate. Ours seems to be a time of transition, and this transition has created much fear and anxiety within the ranks of teachers of the humanities. We see the possibility that younger colleagues will be made jobless, tossed away like the books on the remainder table—employed, if at all, marginally or part-time, underpaid and exploited by the very system that recruited them as graduate students and trained them as teachers and researchers. This fear has both personal and political repercussions for many of us. Yet we are a profession that reads, and the very act of reading is an optimistic act, especially on a cold, dark night of the soul.

Why is it that we do what we do? Why do we spend our time reading, and writing about reading, and teaching about reading? (This is our obsession, even if we extend the idea of reading to other texts, such as film or opera.) As a small child, I hid from the ugliness of urban poverty in the worlds I found in books: they were the space of my extended daydreams, intact worlds in which I felt comfortable and in control. Richard Atwater's classic *Mr. Popper's Penguins* came to be my favorite reading because it was a world in which food, even for penguins, always eventually appeared on the table. Such books served as a refuge from the depressing drabness of city streets and the hopelessness of life on the fringes of the nice world that I spied through my neighbors' window, watching them watching their television set.

As I grew up, the books I read came to reveal less happy, less intact worlds. However, they provided me, in my reverie, with some sense of the pattern of my own world. I learned that in other worlds, such as that of *Huckleberry Finn*, there were other structures, ethics, and morals; these enabled me to start to make sense of the dangers and inadequacies of my own world when federal troops finally integrated the public schools in New Orleans. These books had their fate, and they helped determine mine. When I was a student at university, John Milton and Franz Kafka came along, and then Philip Roth and Günther Grass. I read my way through the sixties into the seventies. My reading stopped being a place into which to flee and became more and more a parallel universe into which I could take myself and my students to help them understand themselves and their world. Social change moved the act of reading into the world of action. Yet people, like books, have their fate. The eighties meant a period of understanding reading as the means by which students could understand their world, through the aesthetic creations of writers (and filmmakers and other creators of texts) who represented the complexities of their own worlds most vividly and most profoundly.

As a teacher of language and literature and culture, I entered into a profession of enthusiasts: few about me complained about the tasks we faced. We wanted to read and write and teach. I joined the MLA as a graduate student, knowing that this was not just a professional organization but an organization of people deeply in love with what we are paid to do, so much so that we often work for less than the minimum wage, commuting from town to town, just to teach, and write, and talk about literature and culture. If I could not support myself through writing and teaching, I would be writing and teaching in addition to whatever it took to earn a living. Today many of our younger colleagues again seem to be confronted with the conflict between what they have trained long and hard to do—what they love to do—and the declining job market.

As a Swiss colleague commented to me last year, we find ourselves, at the millennium, wanting to return to books to hide from the cold and despair of our world. Books, especially for teachers of literature, seem to be a natural refuge from the demons that haunt our world. Although the state of the job market seems to evoke the 1970s, we find ourselves in a very different world. Colleagues call for a return to "literature," or, as the great translator Burton Raffaels stated it, an attempt to "restore . . . the primacy of both literature and intelligence."[1] Pleas for the restoration of literature often seem to regard it as a refuge from our changing times. But these changing times will affect even those who retreat from the cold, harsh realities of the "real world" to the sanctuaries of the MLA and the book.

The attacks on the humanities that I experienced as president of the Modern Language Association in 1995 (and as an officer for the previous two years) were frightening. It is not merely that some colleagues wish to flee into a mythic past but that their fantasies of that past have encouraged demeaning attacks on the best system of higher education in the world, and particularly on the teaching of language, literature, and culture. Higher education was seen as a bastion of left-liberal ideology. It was damned as soft, complacent, smug, and self-satisfied. It was seen as having abandoned "real" values for a quirky relativism. It was a sign of the degeneracy of American society, which was to be rescued by a "return to values." The former Speaker of the House, Newt Gingrich, once an academic himself, roundly condemned the system of higher education that enabled him to achieve his own public success. (Because, like him, I am a Tulanian educated on federal loans and private scholarships, this criticism especially galls me.)

Equally appalling were the attacks on our profession by those in our own fields and institutions. Such relentless attacks on the humanities in general, and the MLA in particular, have given comfort to those whose desire is to diminish and eventually bury our entire system of higher education. Scholars have attacked scholars as the embodiment of the Beast. The number "666" was imagined to be stamped on some of our foreheads by the advocates of other positions. This demonization took place at both ends of the political spectrum. In my discussions during 1995 with the new Republican leadership in Washington, I was dismissed as a self-serving, left-wing relativist. I was also attacked from the left, by scholars such as Cary Nelson, as "self-congratulatory" and giving only lip service as "a defender of the oppressed."[2] The call I heard over and over again was that of the country and western singer Tom T. Hall—hang them all and you'll get the guilty one!

Calls for lowering the decibel level and reintroducing civility into the academic arena have gone unheeded. There are too many who hate civility. Yet all were concerned with the same objects—those books that have their fate—and all were passionate about their concern. The library is burning, and the professors sit around arguing about the color of the books' binding.

In Washington and in many state capitals, a systematic if

often unthinking attempt seems to be under way to dismantle American higher education. With these changes, more and more individuals and groups will be excluded from participation. Thus they will be denied not only the social mobility that education brings but also the experience of the objects that we advocate—books. Middle-class legislators are drawing a line in the sand. "We have made it," they imply, "we had government loans and fellowships to enable us to go to college, and even to graduate or professional school, but we are afraid of our successes being undermined by too many competitors, too many people in the marketplace, too much danger that our children will slip backward into the working class."

The proposed and real reduction of funds for American higher education has resulted in the radical reduction of the size of the professoriate. Fewer full-time professors are being hired; departments and programs are being reduced or closed. Part-time, underpaid, and marginal members of our profession are doing more and more of the teaching. While such changes seem in line with the trend of downsizing in private industry and at the various levels of government, the effect on higher education will have even greater, unforeseen, long-term effects on the social and economic fabric of the United States. In crippling the system of higher education in the United States, those now advocating "downsizing" are assuring a drastic loss in the potential of the American work force and in the intellectual quality of its leadership.

With the breakdown of this system comes a reduction in

the ability of humanists in the modern languages and English to create new knowledge. One of the most productive aspects of the humanities in North America has been the extraordinary explosion of primary research. Fewer scholars are doing more work. As with all primary research, it has the potential of being valuable or being trash. Only time can judge the value of research in the humanities, because what is valuable reveals itself in its application to teaching and the furtherance of new and innovative research. What seems "hot" today may be uninteresting in a decade; what seems marginal today may be the wave of the future. Books really do have their fate. If research support to the humanities is cut off, innovation will be stifled, and our ability to provide the information, tools, and techniques for the next generation of teachers and students will be impeded. We will recycle the research of the past and lose touch with the new questions our students want to ask, questions we need to help them answer. Research in the humanities provides models of thinking and learning: not one model but many, so that our students, some of whom will become our colleagues, can evolve their own way of reading those texts that have their fate. For the rest of our students, it provides models of critical reading and thinking about all texts—different models for different individuals with different needs. Our scholarship reaches outside the academy. I have had letters from physicians who have read my work on medicine and culture and are stimulated enough to write to me about it—often critically!

Recently there has been an outcry against research in

the humanities. "Let them teach and get rewarded for teaching," the chorus sounds. But what are "they" to teach if research does not go on? Is it good teaching to parrot ideas that you yourself have not tested in the public sphere? It is impossible simply to rely on past research for a productive system of higher education. This is as true in the humanities as in the sciences: can you imagine nineteenth-century science still being taught as the state of the art? The loss of jobs in the humanities means the cutting-edge research of the newest academics will be lost to the students of today and tomorrow.

These young scholars add new insights and greater depth to what the academy does. Whether it is teaching students to communicate clearly in English through the written or spoken word or teaching languages other than English, all teachers, beginning and experienced, have a role in the pragmatics of education. And essential to that pragmatic aspect is our research. It may seem esoteric to many, but when we apply it in the classroom we equip students with the ability to do much of what they are supposed to do in our society. The critical, intellectual, and pragmatic skills we teach are what make the archetypal good citizen.

The decline in the academic job market is therefore not merely a problem for those seeking work. Their predicament reflects—and exacerbates—the overall predicament of American society at the end of the twentieth century. Do we want to expand the core of educated society in America—and keep its ranks open to all? Do we want this group to have the critical and pragmatic skills that the humanities provide? I began with Terence on the fate of books (and people) and end with Terence again: *Homo sum; humani nihil a me alienum puto* (as a human being, nothing human is foreign to me). Let us remember civility and kindness and need; let us work together to preserve and improve our profession and our institutions, and seek a common future of books and jobs for all scholars engaged in the task of educating a new elite, drawn from every corner of our society, for the present millennium.

Chapter Five

A HUMANIST

LOOKS AT

LANGUAGE

TEACHING

AND STUDY

A Problem?

We live in a complex moment. In one sense bilingualism has a truly bad press. The common wisdom is that immigrant children should be weaned as quickly as possible from their first language to English so that they can join the mainstream and become real Americans. In the suburbs, however, bilingualism is a good thing. There, kids acquiring a second language are seen as enhancing their earning potential.

It seems that the study of languages has whatever meaning and value you want to give it. Speaking Spanish as a first language in Pilsen, Chicago's Mexican-American community, means that you must learn to speak English to get by; in suburban, wealthy Evanston, it means summers studying in Mexico City or Madrid. Bilingualism is perceived as bad by parents who fear that their kids will be shut out of the American economic system if their first language is primarily Spanish or Polish. (I teach in Chicago, where these are the most important heritage languages!) Bilingualism is necessary, say the parents in the suburbs, to guarantee my kids a place at the top of the new global economy.

Our contemporary dichotomy between language as a burden and language as an advantage seems not at all to be mirrored in the 1979 report *Strength through Wisdom: A Critique of U.S. Capability—A Report to the President from the President's Commission on Foreign Language and International Studies.* Chapter 1 is subtitled: "No longer foreign, no longer alien." Yet in 1999, language has again become both foreign and alien in specific contexts. In 1979, a decade before the end of the cold war, the learning of languages was perceived clearly as a national advantage, and the benefit of learning languages at a young age was the central message of the report. How do you make better Americans in the cold war era? You give them the tools with which they can struggle against the multilingual aggressor. Thus the emphasis of the report is on early language learning—as well it should be.

Yet some attention was also given to higher education. There was a continuation of the older, post-Sputnik, National Defense Education Act model of teaching languages vital to American self-interest. Universities were seen as a pool of language specialists in exotic languages and the site of concomitant language centers that dealt with such languages. In 1979 Persian, Arabic, and Amharic were noted as languages of true national need; today we would (and do) of course list other languages. The need for international studies programs and overseas study programs was also recognized. But such programs were seen as important primarily in the context of national security and economic interests. Indeed, the question of funding such language study was outlined in considerable detail. The Title VI centers in the Department of Education, which supported area and language studies, came to be the realization of the model in the report. The implied ideology was clearly followed over the subsequent decades. It led to a major rupture in the teaching of the "more frequently taught languages" (MFTL) in the United States that has yet to be healed.

From the inception of an advanced teaching model of languages in World War II—in Monterey, California, and Ithaca, New York—language acquisition was pursued for two distinct and very different purposes. Long before World War II the study of languages was perceived as a means of acquiring the command of a "high" culture other than American culture. The teaching of French or German attempted to turn out individuals who could "pass" as French or German in their command of the language and the high culture. (This was very different from the attitude toward Francophone immigrants in Maine, or German immigrants in the Midwest.) Such students went to university and then undertook some study abroad. This model was already in place in the antebellum South, when students from Virginia and Georgia regularly studied in Goethe's Germany.

World War II promoted the notion of an applied and pragmatic knowledge of the language excluding any deep study of cultural objects, except where they provided insight into the mentality of the enemy (or ally). Language was reduced to a means of communication without any claim to deep knowledge. This was possible because there was a large number of "native informants" in virtually all of the relevant languages who had sophisticated knowledge of the culture as well as the language. These two views of language, as special knowledge that ennobles and as pragmatic tool, have persisted in the politics of language study and teaching in American higher education over the past twenty years.

In creating a European studies faculty, the most difficult niche to fill is in the area in the humanities that is the most widely taught: English. Poll the members of any department of English and ask how many are specialists in English culture, and you will find, no matter what their preferred methodology, whether philology or Continental criticism, that most concern themselves with the formal nature of the object or text rather than with its distinctively English expression. (People in Irish studies do quite the opposite.) They are specialists in the novel or the film or material culture or postcolonial studies; the Englishness of their project is, for the most part, incidental to their interest. This is a claim on the "higher" calling of the English department as the place where high (or even mass) culture is studied, not the specific expression of Englishness.

This was also the model in Germanic and Romance departments until the 1990s. With the erosion of interest in Western Europe, a few departments have begun to refurbish themselves as quasi–area studies programs. Yet what they teach and what they study turn out to be just as marginally inflected by the particulars of a national culture as in departments of English. They may teach the German travel narrative of the nineteenth century, but for the most part they do so to understand the universal nature of such narratives, not the particular German need for them or the language in which they are expressed. When teaching on the undergraduate level does attempt to explore the specific nature of the German contribution to a question or a literary form, it is rarely the paradigm offered to graduate student instructors. Their teaching is limited to language, virtually never addressing content, as if this split, underlined by the 1979 report, were a natural one. They are taught to teach the language as an end in itself. Whether aiming at a four-skill fluency or at the reading of canonical texts, the assumption is that graduate students should teach language rather than the complexities of the cultures in which that language is employed. Even those German studies programs that are well structured and take seriously their mandate to explore the widest range of things German (including literature) often do not provide select experience across the curriculum in German for their students.

The 1979 president's commission was one of the key forces in separating the teaching of language, literature, and culture. The guidelines and intentions of the commission were fundamentally positive. They insisted that students should develop usable language skills rather than translation skills for literary analysis or language as a coping mechanism for foreign travel. This emphasis was not, however, necessarily positive for the complex integration of language, textual study, and the use of language in culture. The move to a greater separation of language study and the multiple functions of that study, which would include the study of complex texts of all types, has isolated the traditional literature departments. From my perspective the language and culture movement, perhaps best exemplified in German studies by the work of Claire Kramsch at the University of California at Berkeley, most clearly recognizes the danger of this dichotomy.

For us in the humanities today who take seriously the study and teaching of language, language is both a tool of analysis and also the best object for analysis. The Austrian language critic Karl Kraus made this point a hundred years ago when he simply quoted his opponents, allowing the reader to see them revealed through their very language. The embattled state of most "literature" departments originates from a split vision. Are such departments devoted to the study of literature as an abstraction or to the study of a specific national language—to Goethe or business German?

The idea that the humanities could benefit from the study and teaching of language seems to be losing ground. Language is becoming merely "skills transfer." In most of the Department of Education's Title VI Foreign Language

Area Study (FLAS) programs, language learning is seen as a necessary extension of the social science model. It is simply a skill, like interviewing, that is necessary for serious fieldwork. But it is really understood in a self-reflexive manner, and it is rarely coupled with the importance of written or print culture in such societies. Seeing language as part of the humanities allows the critical humanist to apply analytic tools that enhance the study and teaching of any culture. The humanities, with its complex web of methodological strategies for reading and analyzing complex texts, could provide a natural home for the study of languages. If comparative literature comes to understand itself as the place where textual evidence is examined for multiple purposes and through multiple, comparative modalities (as the late Charles Bernheimer, professor of comparative literature at the University of Pennsylvania, desired), then both the universal claims and the specificity of the national tradition can exist simultaneously.

Humanists do not have a single answer: our approach is just as limited as that of the social scientists. But we recognize that ethical and critical questions arise from the analysis of languages. Humanists can begin to analyze the problematic, cross-cultural meaning of globalized terms such as "human rights." They can question the claim that the goal of the study of language is an "expanding communication among peoples." Humanists of all stripes can help reintegrate the study of literature, culture, and language. It is by using and interrogating such questions that the humanist can contribute.

Restating the Problem

Why do we teach languages at universities? And how? There has been a conflict in the learning and teaching of the more frequently taught languages (MFTL) in the research universities in the United States. On the one hand, graduate education claims to train a new generation of specialist teachers. On the other hand, a department is also expected to teach courses for students outside the major. The undergraduate major was and is seen as producing potential graduate students, and those graduate students were and are seen as the source of the next generation of scholars. "Service" teaching, all teaching that was not focused on actual or potential graduate students, was dismissed as skills transfer.

Happily, over the past decade this imbalance has begun to shift radically. The understanding that the teaching of language is simultaneously the teaching of culture has meant that language courses no longer are seen as service courses but as the prerequisite to more complex levels of cultural and literary analysis. Universities and colleges have also become aware of the need to globalize the undergraduate experience and of the increased importance of the acquisition and use of additional languages. The demands of this increased range of options, as well as economic pressures, have forced educators to look at MFTL as an undertaking in which multiple goals must be pursued. Research universities have begun to examine how a system of higher education can provide structures for the widest range of students, who are interested in MFTL for different reasons. The self-imposed reduction by responsible graduate programs of the number of graduate students in MFTL, due to the reduced job market, has also begun to encourage departments to experiment. (The exception here has been the teaching of Spanish. The number of native and heritage speakers of Spanish, as well as a perception that Spanish is now the second language of the United States, has meant a constant expansion of Spanish instruction even as French, German, and Russian instruction have declined. The growth of interest in Chinese and Japanese, while evident, is not of the same level. And yet many of the same problems exist in the teaching of Spanish as in the other MFTL.)

The more limited the pool of graduate students, the greater the pressure from the faculty to develop interesting teaching opportunities. Students can be attracted into graduate-level courses from other disciplines if such courses make a real attempt to be metadisciplinary. No longer can graduate students expect to teach at research institutions such as the one at which they studied. And the problem of the articulation of graduate education in MFTL and the post–graduate school experience is becoming more and more evident.

The real conflict about goals and intentions that has existed in universities such as Cornell University, between the claims of the Department of Modern Languages and Linguistics (DMLL, as it was constituted up to its dissolution two years ago) and those dedicated departments teaching MFTL, should not be duplicated in any new model. The

DMLL was created during World War II to train intelligence officers in German, Japanese, and other appropriate languages. After the war, it taught virtually all modern languages for undergraduates. (In the past decade it also undertook more instruction in the field of pure linguistics. It has now been divided into a language and a linguistics department.) The language-based departments, such as Romance and German studies, taught upper-division literature and culture courses and trained graduate students in these areas. The focus of the DMLL was on undergraduate teaching; that of the language-based departments was on the training of their graduate students as well as undergraduates who were culturally competent to take their courses. The graduate students saw what went on in the DMLL as outside their interest; the DMLL saw the training of these graduate students, the next generation of teachers of MFTL, as peripheral to their mission. The conflict resulted in a competition between the DMLL and the language-based departments over the philosophy of language learning and teaching.

An Alternative Model

One can teach MFTL in a complex, universitywide structure of *consultation* rather than *competition*. In most of the older language-center models, undergraduate instruction was the sole focus. Graduate students and their training were secondary. Graduate students in turn were exposed to a single, dominant model of the acquisition of the second language and culture that seemed beyond their own scholarly and pedagogic interest. In other research settings with stand-alone departments devoted to MFTL, graduate education predominated, and the teaching of language to undergraduates was understood as a necessary evil to support and train graduate students. All of this accounted for a sense that language teaching was something the good graduate students should be spared.

A different model would address the broader range of language teaching and learning for undergraduates and graduate students. It would provide innovations in language learning without throwing out the baby with the bath water. Research universities have an obligation to retain aspects of the more traditional structure of undergraduate and graduate teaching while acknowledging the realities of the job market and of shifting student interest. A new model for language learning and teaching should benefit not only the widest range of undergraduates but also graduate students who will spend their careers as both teachers and scholars.

The idea is to place MFTL at the center of the university curriculum. While the initial language-learning structures might remain department-based, language instruction in the MFTL after the first or second year could provide instruction analogous to the model of "writing across the curriculum," in which writing becomes a centerpiece of all of the departments in the humanities and social sciences. "Languages across the curriculum" could enable students to study a broad range of topics in ways that seamlessly integrate language instruction. All advanced language courses would also be real "content" courses, motivating the student to apply the use of the language to studying the content of the courses. Both senior faculty members and younger teachers should be involved in teaching these courses, which should address the needs of students in diverse academic settings. Historians of France should be able to do a course in French history in French. These courses could range from the existing culture, literature, and film courses to the teaching of the undergraduate humanities and social science "core courses" in target languages. Thus language could be integrated throughout the undergraduate curriculum. Courses in the humanities (such as philosophy), the social sciences (such as anthropology or government), and possibly the natural sciences could offer discussion sections in languages other than English.

The Role of the Students

Two separate student "pools" of undergraduate language students exist—and each is itself divided into two segments. There are the students who enter university with substantial language experience. They may have had a year or a summer abroad, may have taken advanced placement language courses in high school, or may be heritage or first-generation speakers of another language. These students tend to cluster in a very small number of languages, and particularly Spanish. But while some may see their language skills as central to their college experience, others will regard them as peripheral. For those who want further, specific study in the language and culture, most traditional university departments already offer adequate programs. But for those who wish to undertake preprofessional studies in law, medicine, business, or any other discipline, their language skills may seem marginal to their studies.

On the other hand, more and more students do not begin a second language before university. The older model of a German program, for example, which could rely on students of high school German or heritage speakers to supply the majority of its students, has exhausted itself. For students who will begin their language study at the university, programs must enable them to undertake an intensive experience, including time in the target country, early in their college experience.

Thus language programs must accommodate both students who enter with facility in a language and those who wish to acquire true facility in a language beginning with the university experience. All must incorporate a broader range of courses than the traditional major, and all must offer programs in the target countries.

A related issue is the improvement of language learning in elementary and high schools. The present level of funding for K-12 education in the United States makes it unlikely that language teaching in these grades will improve soon. As with art and music study a few decades ago, language study in many school districts is on the brink of vanishing. For the foreseeable future, universities will bear the primary obligation for the training of students in the MFTL. Strong beginning programs, strong programs abroad, and broader programs of instruction are the answer.

Where Are Languages Taught?

The traditional junior year abroad (JYA) comes too late for undergraduate language instruction. Learning experiences abroad should include freshman core and civilization courses taught abroad, in the contact language; a second-year quarter abroad for beginning language students, with an internship in the field of their interest; the traditional junior year abroad; and internships for juniors and seniors combined with intensive, advanced language instruction. All undergraduates, no matter what their interests, should be able to participate in learning experiences abroad that meet their intellectual and professional goals.

Traditionally, the highly structured nature of science majors (especially premedical programs) has precluded study abroad. While the traditional JYA may well be impossible for such students, a quarter during their first two years (together with a summer internship) might more easily be integrated into the undergraduate experience. If discussion sections were offered in different languages in some of their science and social science courses, such students would be able to maintain their language competence while completing their majors.

Of course, programs abroad are expensive. But the fact that students still pay the full university tuition means that the programs should be self-sufficient. Even if the students are receiving financial aid, the programs abroad should be self-financing. One approach to controlling costs might be to operate collaborative programs run jointly by several colleges and universities. The benefit of having a substantial number of students in residence abroad is also reflected in economies of scale at the home campus. Once a specific percentage of students are studying abroad on a regular basis, the costs on the home campus are reduced, especially those for long-term expansion of facilities.

Programs abroad work only if they are supplemented by adequate, flexible options for language learning and teaching on the home campus. Aside from classroom instruction, language learning can be integrated into living arrangements, with language lounges and houses in the dormitories, as exist in many institutions already. These should be wired for computer and sound equipment to make communication in other languages a constant accompaniment to everyday activities and to enable formal and informal instruction in the living areas. Already projects such as the Iowa-based Scola and the Notre Dame–based RAI project in Italian intend to make ordinary overseas television broadcasts available to students—so that instead of watching *The Simpsons* in their free time, students can tune in to Italian cartoons and sitcoms.

Who Teaches Languages?

Teaching across the curriculum means that teachers of MFTL must prepare courses and materials for a range of options with diverse goals. Research and publication on the teaching of all aspects of the MFTL must be part of this model.

Existing language departments contain scholars of world renown in the study of linguistics, culture, and literature. Already a wide range of courses are offered to undergraduate students interested in a more professional track or who simply enjoy the study of a culture for its own sake. But more instruction should be aimed at students interested in obtaining "real" use of the language in their own fields. This does not mean creating service departments but rather expanding the mission of the teachers of MFTL beyond their present scope.

The new program should offer a wide range of middle-level and advanced courses literally across the curriculum. Discussion sections in MFTL attached to undergraduate courses in biology or macroeconomics should not merely rehearse what has been said in English in German or Spanish; rather they should draw on an analogous German or Spanish textbook or reader in order to teach students how German or Spanish students learn to think about the field. Such sections might be taught by faculty members or by knowledgeable graduate students. Some of these tutors might be graduate students in the specific field with a native or near-native command of the target language. All of these teachers would be closely supervised by second-language acquisition (SLA) specialists in MFTL, who would provide summer workshops to teach them how to teach across the curriculum, provide them with models for testing, and help them develop class plans and educational goals to incorporate both content and language-learning goals. The best computer and language laboratory equipment should be available to both teachers and students.

Speaking Languages Well—Including English

All of the above comments about the teaching of MFTL assume that undergraduate students are native speakers of English, but of course this is not the case. Many students are native or heritage speakers of languages other than English. Courses in MFTL must also take their backgrounds into consideration, providing opportunities for such students to improve their language skills or bring them up to true native ability in courses with real content. But equally important is the teaching of English as a second language, which must be considered as part of the teaching of the more commonly taught languages. ESL for undergraduates means that the best of non–English-speaking undergraduates will have experiences parallel to those of the best students learning other MFTL. Just as any university has entering students with facility in Spanish or German who could benefit from high-level, content-based courses in the target languages, so too we have students whose English, while rated highly on the TOEFL test, could be improved through an experience that uses the language while teaching its nuances. Thus the language laboratory, as it is envisioned in the expanded language center, would deal with the widest range of language learning, including accent modification for speakers of languages other than English as well as teaching pronunciation of MFTL. The language labs should be radically expanded and decentralized. Just as dedicated teaching spaces could exist in classroom buildings and dormitories, so too could there be language lab spaces with state-of-the-art facilities throughout the campus.

The Next Decade

The teaching of MFTL is an imperative for the new university. Arguments about globalization and notions of the special status of the MFTL are not enough. There are probably as many rationales for the teaching and learning of the MFTL as there are cohorts of students. By rethinking languages both within departments dedicated to them and across the entire university, we can address a broader spectrum of needs, and the notion of the need for language instruction will become as unnecessary as the notion of the need for specific writing courses. They simply will be an intrinsic part of all instruction. The goal is to merge the interests of the traditional humanities departments with all of the other claims on the teaching of language. No special pleading is necessary that a humanistic or social science approach to language is "better." All of the goals, from the acknowledgment of the role of high culture to the use of language as a tool to examine the presupposition of cultures, can find a place within the new university, but only if we take seriously the multiaxial notion of language learning and teaching.

Chapter Six

A NEAR FUTURE

PAST THE

MILLENNIUM

German Studies

after 2001

We have concluded a decade of systematic retrenchments in higher education that has permanently changed the profession of university teaching. (In education "permanence" is anything that lasts longer than the limited tenure of a college president—today a bit less than seven years.) As professionals teaching German studies in North America we must be aware of this reality, but it is also important how we "read" it. We can run about crying that the sky is falling (and perhaps it is), but we must also be aware that a large number of positions in German studies could be open but are not. They are still needed to bridge traditional areas of the teaching of language, culture, and literature.

Existing positions have been reduced or eliminated as the need for a "traditional" approach to the teaching of German (preparing undergraduates for graduate training in the area) is seen to have dwindled. Our question now should be: How do we maintain the number and quality of these positions? What can members of the profession do to signal the importance of our field to administrators? (Most of them are from our ranks: we have met the enemy and s/he is us!)

The answer must lie in the value that our undertaking has in our own eyes, as professors teaching about Germany, its history, its culture, its literature, and its language. If we do not respect or understand the significance of our own work in the realm of North American higher education, we will communicate all the wrong messages to those making choices about us, our jobs, and our fields. The rationale of why we should teach German rather than, say, Spanish, Japanese, or Java (the computer language!) is one each generation must decide for itself. After World War II, my generation needed to understand the complex histories of Germany, Austria, Switzerland, and their inhabitants, as well as the often contradictory role that "German" culture played in those histories. The present generation may (must) have other motivations, other interests, such as seeing Germany in the context of a new Europe. There certainly seems to be no reason why German should vanish from among the most commonly taught languages in the United States. Things "German," however defined, still fascinate and challenge us. Indeed, the explosion of American interest in Germany after the collapse of Communism in 1989 and the growing interest in the Shoah more than fifty years after its occurrence are markers of the varied and intense engagement with things German in the United States.

Should we decide to teach German language and culture, we are confronted with a set of presumptions about the institutions in which we will teach. Every institution of higher education is examining itself today in search of greater "productivity" or "efficiency" from its faculty. Increasing costs at both state-funded and private universities (and it is harder and harder to distinguish the two) have driven faculties and administrations to ask hard questions about size of faculty, coverage of programs, and the costs of such undertakings. This self-examination is at an acute stage now, but it has occurred in many areas of higher education over the past few decades, even in the boom years of the 1980s. There has, however, been a sea change in the arguments—and the methods—employed.

The contested decision at Bennington College in 1995 marked the transition between the older model of cutting programs and a rather frightening newer model. Elizabeth Coleman, the president of Bennington, fired twenty-six of its seventy-nine professors whose teaching, she declared, had grown stale. She also eliminated academic divisions and a few departments, including all of the foreign-language teaching staff, even those with "presumptive tenure," long-term employment at the college.

Over the decades programs have been regularly cut at

universities. My institution, the University of Chicago, recently closed its historically important department of education, founded by John Dewey, when it was felt that the department could no longer meet national standards of excellence. Washington University did the same with its sociology department. The State University of New York at Albany closed its German department. Other institutions of high learning have regularly closed programs, including those in foreign languages, because of financial exigency.

In none of these other cases was the basis of the decision that there was a general problem with teaching a specific field at universities and colleges. Each closing was the result of the local situation. Coleman's take on the situation was quite different. The foreign language staff with and without presumptive tenure were dismissed because it was argued that the teaching of foreign languages was merely skills transfer (like the teaching of typing) and that this was not a proper task for colleges and universities. Indeed, Coleman asserted that a regional language-learning center based in a local high school could easily fulfill the needs of Bennington students for language instruction. This argument sadly echoes the view inculcated in graduate students in many Ph.D.-granting departments: bear with language teaching at the beginning of your career; once you get tenure you won't have to bother with it. Because so few graduate students are exposed to the intellectual rationale of language teaching as the teaching of culture, most of them, too, regard it as skills transfer. There are major exceptions, but the emphasis on the teaching of "high" literature to the exclusion of language and culture by the research institutions has underwritten this attitude.

Jobs vanish. The existing system seems to valorize the elimination of such jobs or the turning over of language instruction to part-time faculty, untrained "native informants," or, most egregiously, undergraduates. Rather than stress that the teaching of language in all of its complexities is a job for professionals, some colleges use undergraduates to lead the drill sessions and offer supplemental teaching. The pedagogical rationale is that undergraduates can teach language just as well as graduate students, because all that is considered necessary (beyond some basic proficiency) is enthusiasm. In a sense that is true, since few research institutions provide the rationale for language teaching; yet most have been forced to train their teaching assistants rigorously because of the complaints of undergraduates and their parents. These undergraduates are rarely as well trained as even the beginning graduate TA. What is most important is that their services are cheap: indeed, in some institutions they are paid with credits toward a degree that they have paid real money to earn. They are cheaper than even part-timers or untrained native informants. And, unlike many faculty members, they are often enthusiastic about their participation in such programs!

Such attitudes toward the instruction of language reinforce the Bennington argument. If undergraduates can do it, why do we need faculty members? Eventually we can scrap the whole thing—purge language instruction of faculty participation and turn it over to self-instruction. With a good computer program, runs this argument, you can learn Japanese just as you learn typing!

Not only does this attitude limit the number of new jobs that can and will be created in modern languages, but it also places the very notion of teaching languages in jeopardy. Many of us de facto participate in the rationale behind this reduction in faculty lines. When a Spanish department can fill all its upper-division courses it seems superfluous to spend faculty time on introductory Spanish— and therefore it becomes difficult, if not impossible, for entering students to receive competent instruction in beginning Spanish. In the 1990s the University of California at Berkeley attempted to banish its beginning Spanish students to night school. However, after students protested, this approach was quickly abandoned and beginning language instruction resumed in the "normal" offerings of the department.

Part-time faculty, adjunct faculty, and then no faculty are and will continue to be employed in such systems. German departments do not have this luxury. "Can't you just hire a couple of undergraduates to monitor the auto-tutorial in German?" asks the dean. "That would save us the part-time budget line. We'll give them credit for an upper-level language pedagogy seminar." Academic administrators now look toward the day when language instruction will be carried out with interactive video, without even the presence of undergraduate monitors. Shades of the 1960s, when the language laboratory was going to free everyone from the rote teaching of language.

Language teaching is the teaching of culture in complex and direct ways. In 1995, the year I was president of the MLA, Sam, our twelve-year-old, began German in seventh grade at the Lab School. His first lesson was learning titles: *Herr, Frau, Fräulein*. The textbook pointed out that the equivalent for "Ms." in German was *Frau*. This was an observation on both German culture's understanding of gender roles and that of the American speaker of English, one Sam understood immediately. This cultural lesson—unintended and unplanned—occurred on his very first day. Teaching language is teaching culture; teaching culture is teaching history, and teaching history is teaching literature. All of these come together in the new vistas open for German studies in North America. Yes, add gender, class, and race to the curriculum; expand courses to teach film and colonial and postcolonial studies—but don't forget the teaching of language as a cultural experience as part of our future.

To assure new jobs, to assure the continuation of old positions in the teaching of foreign languages, we must place a new emphasis on language teaching in training our graduate students and rewarding our colleagues. While administrators speak of internationalization (in the name of new revenue sources), they must recognize that the teaching of languages and of culture in those languages cannot be turned over to the ubiquitous proprietary language schools or some long-awaited new technology. Language teaching, and the teaching of languages and cultures, is an intrinsic part of American higher education. Through such instruction students gain new understanding of American language and culture as well as of the "target" culture. Teaching language is the ground on which all further work must be undertaken. In demanding that jobs in foreign languages be maintained, let us at the same time look to our own sense of the role that we as German studies teachers play in higher education.

HOW TO PRESERVE THE TEACHING OF GERMAN LANGUAGE AND CULTURE IN TWENTY MINUTES

UNDERGRADUATE INSTRUCTION

• Make sure that your language teaching teaches culture. Aim toward some real-life experience with the language in a program abroad, whether it is a sophomore quarter, a summer internship, or a junior year abroad

• Teaching undergraduates demands diversity. Teach courses in German as well as in English; give lecture courses as well as small seminars; offer courses for freshmen with senior faculty; encourage faculty to get involved with weekend seminars for high-school students.

• Offer courses with and for the broadest range of undergraduates with colleagues across the disciplines. Make sure German courses are cross-listed in other disciplines; make sure you coteach with colleagues from other departments. Offer courses that reflect the strengths of your faculty. Don't offer courses merely "because we have to."

• Concentrate not on the number of German majors but

on the range of students in your courses. The more diversity your courses offer, the more good students you will have. Stress joint majors and certificates in German for social science students as well as traditional and innovative programs for the German major.

• Be aware of what your students will teach and research after they leave you. Don't make them reinvent themselves when they are out in the real world. Chronological coverage of all periods and texts is not the only model; focused programs can be just as effective in articulating graduate studies with postgraduate work experience.

• As with undergraduate courses, figure out what the faculty in your graduate program can teach, and build your program around their academic and research strengths, not around some abstract notion of what "must" be taught.

• Admit small numbers—no more than two or three graduate students a year. Be very selective while respecting diversity. Weed seriously after the first year. Offer adequate support, so that five years is sufficient to complete a doctoral program. Limit your expectations to what can actually be accomplished in five years.

• Offer teaching internships rather than teaching assistantships. Teach graduate students how to teach in all areas, not just language. Create work experiences in other arenas at the university: film series, music series, the art museum, as well as summer experiences in industry and government (through alumni).

ADMINISTRATION

• Don't count heads in single courses; look at the total enrollment in a program over a year. Language courses must be small to be effective. However, lectures don't have to be.

• Support programs abroad. Make this a permanent attraction of your institution. Provide leadership for the internationalization of American academe. Provide exchanges for students and faculty with schools and universities abroad.

• Scholarship fuels teaching at *all* institutions. With no original scholarship people quickly revert to teaching their graduate school notes, an approach that palls (for both teacher and students) after a few years. Support original, peer-reviewed research as part of the mission of teaching. Support faculty participation in summer institutes such as those sponsored by the NEH or DAAD. Encourage these activities with promotions and leaves.

• Respect your faculty. Don't hire part-time faculty to replace full-time, committed faculty. In research universities, regard teaching assistantships not as inexpensive labor but as internships. Make teaching assignments flexible.

Advocates of abandoning the study of Germany, its language, and its culture as superfluous in the next century run the risk of forgetting the past and ignoring the future. The complexity of the "German" past, from Kant to Goethe to Freud to Hitler to Dix to Schoenberg, is central to any understanding of how we, as North Americans, have been shaped. Things "German" have formed us (even those of us without genealogical roots in Central Europe) and continue to do so. But a significant part of our future in North America lies in our relationship to the new Europe and the Berlin Republic, that new Germany which has served and most probably will continue to serve as the commercial and technical engine of Europe. Here our study of older models, such as the meaning, role, and ideology of science and medicine in Germany in the past, can provide us with some insight into how a national state can define itself even without emphasizing its national identity. German studies is a test case for the permeability of an area-study model in and by disciplinary interests. "Germany" (along with Austria and Switzerland) and the "Germans"—however defined—will remain a power in our understanding of the world and ourselves. Let us do it right!

Chapter Seven

GERMAN?

AMERICAN?

LITERATURE?

Some Thoughts

on the Problem

of Question Marks

and Hyphens

My concern with German studies has focused on Germany and Austria as the locations of the history and culture that fascinate me. As an American scholar of German studies I had somehow lost track of how much the interpenetration of German and American culture had shaped my own desire to look at this area. And yet my concern with American ethnic writing, evidenced by the special issue on ethnicity that I guest-edited for the *PMLA* (no. 113, January 1998), moved me to rethink the role that German culture has had in the United States from colonial times to the present. It also led me to remember my own graduate education.

In the early 1960s I took two seminars on "German-American Literature" from John T. Krumpelmann, an emeritus professor from Louisiana State University. Krumpelmann had written his dissertation in 1924 at Harvard on the translator and cultural mediator Bayard Taylor (1825–1878), a thesis that was published only in 1959.[1] His claim to fame was his little book on southern scholars in Goethe's Germany.[2] His approach to German American writing seemed pedestrian to me even in 1961. What he did in class and in numerous essays (lists, rather) was to tabulate the initial appearance of Americanisms in the work of German-language writers such as Charles Sealsfield or Otto Ruppius. This I certainly did not find interesting even as philology.

I realize now, decades later, in trying to rethink the very category of "German American writing," that Krumpelmann's approach, like that of his contemporaries in the 1930s and 1940s, such as Harold Jantz at Johns Hopkins, was to stress the Americanization of German writing. At that time, the idea of "tribes and peoples" originated by the Viennese Germanist Josef Nadler was being explicitly politicized by Nadler's Austrian compatriot Heinz Kindermann.[3] He stressed that German writing on the margins and abroad (*Grenzdeutsche Literatur* and *Auslandsdeutsche Literatur*) was inherently and purely German. It was almost archaic in its Germanness. It was a racially pure literature that remained pure even under the threat of acculturation. American critics from the 1930s to the 1950s reacted by stressing that German American writing was as much American as it was German. They placed these texts, at

least the canonical texts, between the two worlds and beyond the world of race theory. It was also no accident that
such critics chose as their objects antiauthoritarian German writers in the United States such as Charles Sealsfield
or Friedrich Gerstäcker.

But the philological bent of such academic critics, combined with the growing antiquarianism and parochialism
of the "official" publications of German-American (note
the hyphen) literature, pushed this field to the margins of
both German and American studies. The status of other
ethnic literary traditions in the United States, such as Nor-
wegian American literature, and of other forms of German
culture in a German diaspora, as in Brazil, show much the
same decline into *Heimatliteratur* and parochialism. German
studies (and even *Germanistik*) found such literary texts
neither "high" enough nor compelling enough for placement within even the most expanded canon. Rarely did
such texts appear in "serious" scholarship.[4] But after 1968,
the notion of an anticanon evolved in German studies,
first in Germany and then in the United States, carried, as
we shall see, by the latest wave of German intellectual immigrants. Suddenly, "popular" writers such as Karl May,
whose early twentieth-century novels about the "Wild
West" still shape German notions of America, appeared as
objects of scholarly interest. A few eyes even turned to the
more canonical German American writers such as the authors of the American frontier, Gerstäcker and Sealsfield.
Historians of *Alltagsgeschichte* discovered another form of
writing from America, the letters and diaries of German

immigrants. Perhaps the best volume is that published in English under the title *News from the Land of Freedom: German Immigrants Write Home.*[5] Such texts produced by non-literary writers were initially "mined" for facts about daily life among German immigrants, but soon feminist critics and historians noted that they also provide insight into questions of identity and experience. Recently Linda Schelbitzki Pickle has used such materials with great subtlety.[6] Do such appropriations of "popular" or "archival" texts make an implicit claim, which has its own history? Do they not implicitly claim that such texts are truer in grasping the German experience than the study of "high" literature? These were often the very literary texts (besides the Bible, in its various versions) read by their authors.

Another result of examining archival texts such as diaries and letters is that the politics of German American culture seems to be conservative if not reactionary. With the exception of antislavery texts and a small number of studies of the German radical left, such as Carol Poore's, little has been done with texts on the left.[7] This is not because they are unknown. Karl J. R. Arndt has catalogued dozens of left-wing journals and newspapers.[8]

Between 1968 and the 1980s, German-American literature as heritage studies became more and more the stepchild of American German studies. If any work in this area was taken seriously, it was work by historians such as my colleague Kathleen Conzen on the construction of German-American identity in Milwaukee[9] and a small number of feminist studies, such as the work of Linda

Pickle. But these books can be counted on the fingers of one hand.

Starting in the 1960s, however, German studies has harbored an ever more active field of "exile" studies, which examines the German Jewish diaspora in the United States as well as elsewhere in the world. It was driven heavily by Jewish scholars, many of them German Jews such as Günther (Guy) Stern, and disaffected German, non-Jewish liberal academics who came to the United States in the 1960s and 1970s. The real split was between the heritage approach to German American writing, which claimed to deal with regional "German" (read: non-Jewish) writing, and the literature of (Jewish) victimhood, the study of "exile," encompassing even writers who chose to remain outside Germany after 1945. One could also measure this split by who did the work: German American apologists saw themselves as defending a conservative cultural tradition defamed by American attitudes toward the Germans from 1914 to 1945; students of "exile" literature saw themselves as the real victims of the reactionary politics of many of these Germans during the same period. The former saw themselves as the rooted exponents of a real German tradition in American culture (however defined); the latter, following the lead of George Steiner, among others, defined exile as a condition of writing. One might add that the former stressed the "healthy" nineteenth-century (i.e., pre–World War I) roots of German American culture; the latter had little or no interest in American German culture before 1933 and therefore ignored the culture into which German Jews entered after 1933.

The more antiquarian the exponents of German American writing became, the less scholarship, on the wider level, took note of them. Recently, in her volume of interviews *Tearing the Silence*, Ursula Hegi raised the question of the continuity of German (i.e., non-Jewish) experience after the Shoah.[10] (Hegi gained mass popularity when her Günther-Grass–like novel *Stones from the River* was selected as one of the titles for Oprah Winfrey's TV book club.) Young Germans who, like Hegi, had come to the United States in their teens revealed that they had crafted their American identity around their guilt as Germans.[11] But what is striking about Hegi's volume of carefully recrafted essays is the perpetuation of the dichotomy between Germans and Jews, one that haunts contemporary German writing on the topic even when that writing is in English. (Here I can mention the "philo-Semitic" autobiography by Björn Krondorfer, a young German-born historian now teaching in the United States, who wrote a participant-observer study of encounters between young Jews and Germans.)[12] The young Jews are American Jews. (As everyone knows, America is the real Jewish country, or at least New York is the Jewish city. Forget Israel and Jerusalem; it is easier to be a German philo-Semite in the United States!) Hegi's volume simply elides the presence of Jews in Germany today and among the Germans who now live and work in the United States. Certainly all scholars in my field can easily evoke the names of German Jewish scholars such as Liliane Weisberg or Miriam Hansen or Y. Michal Bodeman. Hegi's volume, which closes with an interview with

"Katharina, born 1947, age at time of immigration 10," is titled "When Germans and Jews Can Talk." The idea of being both Jewish and German seems contradictory. The
shadow of the Shoah and the feeling or rejection of guilt is
found in all of Hegi's interviews. But the voice of the German Jew is missing; German Jews, if they did not die in
Auschwitz, show up in America only as older refugees
among whom these young Germans must live. They are not
their peers. This blind spot marks the mutual exclusion of
things German and things Jewish in America—an antipathy
as powerful among Germans as among Jews who refuse to
drive a Volkswagen (even though many of these Jews still
see themselves as Jews with a German Jewish ancestry).

Among some German academics who came to the
United States, identification with the victim—or the trans-
mutation of guilt into a form of victimhood—lies at the
core of their own work. Most of this work has been positive, even though the identification of German economic
immigrants of the 1960s with the lot of the refugees and
victims of the Nazis was often strained. The refugees,
among them Oscar Seidlin, professor of German at Ohio
State, and Heinz Politizer, at the University of California at
Berkeley, were hard at work creating an idealized world of
German culture that they, in their American exile, had rescued from the Nazis. In spite of Seidlin's work for the
OSS, such critical writing was little inflected by an interest
in the recuperation of a German American culture. Only
in the past decade have younger left-wing critics such as
Frank Trommler (in his work in rescuing the German Li-

brary in Philadelphia), and Peter Uwe Hohendahl (as president of the Heine Society, rebuilding the Heine Fountain in New York City), discovered themselves as German Americans. This discovery is equally apparent in Ruth Klüger's brilliant memoir of her survival in Auschwitz and her entry into (German Jewish) American society in the late 1940s.[13] In such works a dialogue has begun to develop among and between groups. Being German in America has come to be expressed in ever more complex ways and within complex actions. Identification has enabled individuals to grow through a sense of a communal activity with the other group.

As Marx notes, tragedy, when recycled, becomes parody. Perhaps the most amazing appropriation of the model of guilt and victimhood is in the recent work by Timothy J. Holian, *The German-American and World War II: An Ethnic Experience*, and in the "documentation" published by the *German American Yearbook*'s editor Don Heinrich Tolzmann.[14] These texts, so ably analyzed by Jeffrey Sammons, reveal a desire to hop on the victims' bandwagon, to create a "Holocaust" (their word, not mine) of German Americans during the early 1940s.[15] These authors aspire to the victim status appropriately claimed by West Coast Americans of Japanese ancestry interned at Manzanar and other camps. But their real need is to create a status analogous to that of the "exile" writers and their academically acceptable critics as serious objects of study.

I want to argue for a continued reconciliation of "German American" and "Jewish" writing along a model entrenched in American historiography: the model of the frontier. We are at a point where these older categories of the German American have outlived their usefulness and have become parodies of themselves. We must reconceptualize the notion of a German culture in America, and to do so we can adopt the model of the frontier now widely accepted in the field of the new Western history.

Stephen Aron notes that the "new Western history" began with Patricia Limerick's casting off of Turner's notion of the frontier as an "unsubtle concept for a subtle world." But, as Aron argues quite correctly, the frontier remains at the center of the new field: "Rather than banishing the word for past offenses, western historians need to make the most of the frontier. Reconfigured as the lands where separate polities converged and competed, and where distinct cultures collided and occasionally coincided, the frontier unfolds the history of the Great West in ways that Turner never imagined."[16] Turner, who used the idea of the frontier to define his understanding of America, would not recognize the concept as it is applied today. For North American historians it is the new "F" word, according to Kerwin Lee Klein, one that may present problems in constructing a new regionalism at the expense of a national identity.[17] However, it is the ability to balance the moment of the frontier experience with the general sense of an integrative history of peoples that makes the frontier a useful category for the writing of the German American cultural history.

Recent discussions of the imagined border, as in the work of Gloria Anzaldúa, have tended to romanticize the border as an ideal space of meeting and merging.[18] But the border can also be a locus of competition that leads to destruction and to massacres, to the commission of acts abominable in the eyes of all parties: banishment, rape, and murder. The destruction of the Amalechites, of the Jews of England, of the Native Americans in the *pays d'en haut* all occurred at frontiers. In this liminal space all parties are forced to understand and define themselves in the light of their experience of the Other. And liminality is not always rewarded by the approval of the marginal, or by its movement to a new center with the forces of power at the periphery.

Richard White's writing about the frontier can serve as a model for such a history. White's greatest historical work is *The Middle Ground*.[19] This work began as a rather straight rewriting of North American Native American history in the *pays d'en haut*—lower Canada and the adjacent British colonies to the south—in the eighteenth century. White, too, was surprised when he found the frontier a useful concept. In his detailed, often horrific, often fascinating, account, he develops the idea of a space of contestation and accommodation. His idea of the frontier as the "middle ground," the space of compromise, is helpful in shaping a new vision of the role of Germans, however defined, in American cultural history.

The potential values and horrors of the compromise position are revealing: the confrontation between and among cultures and peoples can provide a new, multivocal account of the histories of a people. The frontier as imagined by

White is not a pure space, an absolute answer to the center/periphery model of history. White's model is an attenuated center/periphery model that focuses on the distance from the presumptive center as a factor in the ability of the "middle ground" to serve as a place of accommodation and confrontation. Yet the center (in White's account of the Great Lakes region from 1650 to 1815, London or Paris) truly vanishes. The real marker of the middle ground is the language spoken. Certainly English and French are the contesting languages, but the wide range of Native American tongues dominates his account. Indeed, his marker of the mediator is the "hybrid," which he defines as the offspring of Europeans and Native Americans. In point of fact, the true "hybrids," to use the term most favored in postcolonial theory, are those who can negotiate between languages. Language is the marker of hybridity as well as the source of conflict.

In the German experience in the United States, from the seventeenth-century antislavery author Francis D. Pastorius to my colleagues Ruth Klüger and Frank Trommler, we see an analogous tale of complexity and contestation, of assimilation and self-consciousness. Let us break down the categories that compete for the highest level of integration or victimhood. Let us see how groups coming out of an ever-shifting "German" cultural realm, whether Lutherans, Catholics, Jews, or Freethinkers, "Aryans" or "Jews," "Bavarians" or "Prussians," educated (*gebildet*) or uneducated, compete to create communities and cultures. In doing so, we must broaden our notion of texts. Archival letters and diaries are no more valid in such a context than are memoirs or belles-lettres. Of course, in addition to high literature, mass and popular literature must be included, along with the preaching and liturgy of many of these groups.

We must avoid the desire to homogenize a single German experience at this frontier. Conflicts emerged among groups within the constructed notion of the "German"—which excluded the "Jew" after 1871. Yet Jews from Germany and Austria (German-speaking or not) strongly identified themselves as "Germans." Emancipated Jews from the early nineteenth century to the 1930s (and beyond) saw themselves as belonging to the German cultural sphere. Now, we can argue whether Gershom Sholem was right or whether Dan Diner is right in speaking about an illusion of symbiosis or a negative symbiosis;[20] we can debate whether or how the Germans saw and see Jews as Germans. But we cannot dispute that this cultural tension existed. This powerful identification with German culture is dramatically different from the general orientation of Jews in Russia, Poland, or the Soviet Union, although it is similar to that of Jews from Hungary.[21] Jewish writers and thought must be reintegrated into German American studies.

But such a cultural history must not be bound by language. "German American literature" must not be restricted to writing in German. A commonplace about Saul Bellow is that his novels are incomprehensible outside the tradition of Yiddish culture. It is not that he writes in Yiddish but rather that he was shaped by the world of secular, left-wing Yiddish culture. (And, I can add, he was thereby moved to translate I. B. Singer's brilliant short story "Gimpel the Fool" for *Esquire*, bringing that American writer into the mainstream of American letters.) The contested notion of German culture must also make a place for writers such as H. L. Mencken (with all of his private anti-Semitic views) and Theodore Dreiser. The former had a clear debt to the German newspaper essay, and the latter's relationship to German realism is self-evident.

There is also a moment when German culture in America is defined as Jewish culture. There is a sense of the continuity of belonging to a constructed cultural sphere, even with the shift in language. Thus Emma Lazarus, herself an American Jew of Sephardic background, not only wrote *Alide: An Episode of Goethe's Life* (1874), but her translations of Heinrich Heine's poems, beginning in 1881, also shaped the poetic voice of the author of "The New Colossus." The boundary between German culture, Jewish culture, and American culture is permeable, and this factor must be acknowledged in redefining all three literary canons.

Let me take a very recent example: Peter Fröhlich's autobiographical *My German Question: Growing Up in Nazi Berlin*.[22] Peter Fröhlich is better known as the intellectual historian Peter Gay. He is a member of the "child immigrant" generation of Jews from Germany, often dubbed the "Kissinger generation," which has done so much to shape American public consciousness over the past half century. They were often middle-class youngsters, spoiled rotten, who suffered a radical displacement into the marginal world of the refugee. They were not, as Gay himself is at pains to stress, child survivors, as was the German Jewish novelist Jurek Becker. Rather, they were children who escaped incarceration in the camps and came to America young enough to assimilate into American culture but old enough to retain powerful emotions about their trauma. Their escape marked them in complex ways, different from the ways in which child survivors' experiences marked them. The child immigrants had been at risk; they had family (as Gay did) who died in Nazi prisons and concentration camps; they experienced a radical disruption of their middle-class lives. The Jewish middle class in Germany had also gone through economic displacement in the hyperinflation of the 1920s. But this radical alteration of their economic status, as Gay shows, did not change their feeling that they were part of a German cultural and economic world. A German proverb notes that "suffering shared is suffering halved." Middle-class Jews were neither better nor worse off than others who suffered in the worldwide economic collapse. Indeed, their common experience reinforced their sense of belonging.

Speaking of a "Jewish" middle class is itself rather complicated. Gay stresses in his account of his first decade how little his family felt themselves to be "Jewish." He muses, "Jewish awareness? Jewish identity? These were empty slogans to [his parents]—and then to me. . . . When as an adolescent I declared that if I were ever to get married, it would be to a gentile, I was only pushing to its limits my parents' uncompromising rejection of any tribal identification" (49). The great European historian George Mosse, a

German Jew of a much different economic class (his father owned the German equivalent of the *New York Times*), has written about "German Jews beyond Judaism," and that image certainly works for Gay's view of his own family. Rescuing this secular, German Jewish tradition from opprobrium is the overt purpose of his autobiography.

Gay attempts to put to rest the myth that German Jews were so blinded by their Germanness that they could not see what was happening to them. He makes this point repeatedly to explain why he is writing this account of his childhood. Alan Bullock, the great British biographer of Hitler (and of Stalin), discusses the two historical models that have attempted to explain the Shoah. The first assumes that the murder of the Jews of Europe was part of Hitler's plan from his dictation of *Mein Kampf* in 1925–26 and that one had to be blind (or at least illiterate) to not have anticipated the "final solution" from the very beginning of Nazi hegemony. The second assumes that the movement toward the Shoah was down a slippery slope: that it began with the disenfranchisement of the Jews and their economic and social isolation. With the press of the war, with the invasion and conquest of Poland and much of Central and Eastern Europe, the Shoah became the only option seen by German leadership after 1941 to resolve the "Jewish question."

Gay is a partisan of the latter view. Nobody he knew initially took the Nazis seriously as threatening the civil rights of the Jews, since virtually no one actually read *Mein Kampf*. In the world he inhabited, the unchanged, Wilhelmine institutions of the grammar school and the high school (*Gymnasium*), such topics were hardly mentioned even by the most rabid Nazi sympathizer after 1933. But Gay acknowledges the different experience of other Jewish children who remained in non-Jewish schools after 1935. Indeed, the preponderance of memoir literature speaks against Gay's benign memories of his school days. It documents a growing hostility to Jews, especially in the high bourgeois institutions such as the elite schools. Most Jewish children were withdrawn or expelled from the school system (as, eventually, was young Peter Gay). Economic isolation meant social isolation as well. Certainly, and Gay documents one salient case, there were non-Jews who were willing, indeed eager, to maintain their relationships with their Jewish friends. But the experience of most, and Gay documents this without saying it, was that non-Jews abandoned their colleagues and neighbors not by aggressive anti-Semitic acts but simply by ignoring them. As more laws were promulgated to make them visible, the Jews in Germany became in fact more invisible. They could be and were ignored as if they did not exist. For every employee who hid family silver, to use Gay's example, there was a businessman whose denunciatory actions disenfranchised his Jewish colleagues, as in the tale Gay tells of his father's partner.

But what is Peter Gay's underlying memory of his own youth? He knows, as we do, that all such memories are selective, but memories of what? This is the central question of a memoir that concludes by asking how Gay came to be interested in psychoanalysis. Gay's memoir reveals to his reader much more about what being "Jewish" came to mean. As I have noted, in defining his family as Jews Gay dismisses all religious practices. His family had a Christmas tree and looked down on relatives who were "three-day-a-year Jews," going to temple on the high holidays, Rosh Ha-Shonah and Yom Kippur. Ritual seemed unimportant. Gay was circumcised as a child, but he questions (in a manner very reminiscent of his parents' generation and our own) whether this was a ritual choice or a medical one. Gay clearly also dismisses any identification of Jews as Zionists. His father was a Social Democrat, no more or less so because he was a Jew. Nor was Jewishness a social identity, such as the shared obsession with sports. Gay's obsession with sports, especially soccer, was common to all divisions of German society. He belonged to a Jewish boy scout group, but he sees this identity as separate from his love of sports.

And yet there was no question of conversion. Gay and his family remained Jews. In this way, Gay's life paralleled that of Sigmund Freud, the subject of his great biography. Freud was seen as a "godless Jew," but he believed those who abandoned their identities as Jews were either without character or psychopathic. But if it was not religion or politics or social identity, then what was it that shaped Gay's idea of the "Jew"?

The central factor in all of the discussions of Jewishness that Gay provides is the physical nature of the Jew. Jews are different from non-Jews, according to the ideology of science that dominated European and American thought from the close of the nineteenth century through the 1940s, because they are a different race. Jews look different, and the difference written on the body reveals the difference of character and mind. (This was a powerful theme in Voltaire's view of the Jews; Voltaire is the subject of one of Gay's other major works.)

The Jewish body, then, was defined as different by the world in which Gay grew up. But you could hide. His father, "people said, 'did not look Jewish.' . . . He was a good-looking man, with blue eyes, a straight nose, and slightly wavy hair combed back straight à la Goethe" (23). His deceitful, non-Jewish business partner, on the other hand, looked too Jewish. "Several customers [told] my father that he would do well to get rid of the Jew Pelz and thus improve his business" (75). He was surrounded by Jews who, like his *Tante* Esther, "had handsome, delicate features and stunning long blond hair: it is one of the appalling ironies of my family history that she, whom the Nazis later murdered in an extermination camp, was assigned the role of Germania in a school play" (25). His parakeet, "a blue little bird . . . with its curved beak, I told myself ruefully, even looked Jewish" (18).

The Jewish body comes to be different for Gay. In his memories, young Peter passes as a non-Jew. "I had blue eyes and a straight nose, like my parents, I did not 'look Jewish.' . . . I judged my appearance to be just as it should be . . . a case of boyish narcissism, perhaps (I am ashamed even to think this) fed by the official propaganda touting the Teutonic looks that were, according to nazi ideology, the ideal" (57).

In his memoir Gay lives out what defined the Jew in his world: the body of the Jew. His obsession with sports and his youthful anxiety about sexuality seem in his narrative to reflect his guilt about his identification with the aggressor. This fantasy about the Jewish body stands at the center of Gay's memories as it does in the 1920s memoir by the famed German Jewish author Jakob Wassermann (1873–1934). Wassermann also chronicled the ambivalence of the German Jews toward their own bodies. He wrote: "I have known many Jews who have languished with longing for the fair-haired and blue-eyed individual. They knelt before him, burned incense before him, believed his every word; every blink of his eye was heroic; and when he spoke of his native soil, when he beat his Aryan breast, they broke into a hysterical shriek of triumph."[23] In consequence, Wassermann argues, Jews came to feel disgust for their own bodies. Even when these bodies were identical in *all* respects to the bodies of Aryans, they perceived a difference: "I was once greatly diverted by a young Viennese Jew, elegant, full of suppressed ambition, rather melancholy, something of an artist, and something of a charlatan. Providence itself had given him fair hair and blue eyes; but lo, he had no confidence in his fair hair and blue eyes: in his heart of hearts he felt that they were spurious." This doubt too is part of the hidden message of Peter Gay's memoir.

Once this anxiety about the authenticity of the body is seen, the question of what made Gay "Jewish" can be answered. And this answer reflects on whether German Jews were conscious of the possibility of their own destruction.

The anxiety about the Jewish body, as reflected in the caricatures of Julius Streicher's newspaper *Der Stürmer*, predates 1933. Gay's anxiety about his identification with those whom he seemed to resemble was a reflex of his belief that in his own mind he could not "look Jewish." Because of Gay's identification with the aggressor, in his fantasy he was both perpetrator and victim. He was Jewish and not Jewish simultaneously. This double bind accounts for the extraordinary but appropriate anger in his memoir: not the anger he recounts toward his controlling parents, but toward Streicher and his "German" image of the Jew, which haunts the pages of this memoir. When he lists the Nazis hanged after the Nuremberg trial, he notes: "And last but by no means least, Julius Streicher—I have mentioned him before but I don't mind mentioning him again in this context—[was] hanged" (187).

How does this powerful emotion about being labeled as "Jewish" in spite of looking "German" reflect on the self-consciousness of the present-day emeritus professor of history? Gay stresses that this is a selective memoir, one that concentrates only on the first decade of so of his life, and then only on his experiences in Nazi Germany. Gay emphasizes his pampered upbringing: "Every day I had been good, which meant every day, I would trundle over to a nearby bakery and get my treat. After six decades I still literally salivate at the memory" (34). And in his later years, he notes with irony, he has developed type II diabetes, which precludes his eating the chocolate and whipped-cream *Mohrenkopf*. But Gay literally disavows in this memoir any Proustian connection, stating that he had no such visceral connection to his earlier experience, no madeleine. But the cake and the diabetes point to the hidden Jewish body: diabetes was nicknamed "the Jewish disease" in Germany. Gay's question of what made him Jewish can be answered by this enduring sense of the Jewish body, the body that was not seen as Jewish but which betrayed itself. It is a striking testimony to the power of the internalization of images in understanding oneself.

Gay's memoir is staged as part of his understanding of how he became an American. The universals that Gay can espouse are clearly drawn from this account. No American, Gay's worldview implies, can be defined by his or her body—ignoring the importance of race in the United States. Diabetes is not a "Jewish" disease but a disease of the aging body. In the United States from the 1940s to the present, for good or for ill, it is the body that defines race first and foremost. But Jews in the United States are white and healthy—or so they imagine themselves. They do not appear different—or so they hope. The universal of sport binds people in the United States together as it did (in the memory of Peter Gay) the Germans, both Jews and Aryans.

But of course the America to which Peter Fröhlich came saw Jews as different. Indeed, like Gay, Jews saw themselves as different. The analytic work of the Harvard psychologist Gordon Allport (1897–1967) in 1946, followed by a series of papers in the late 1950s, attempted to understand what was being measured when Jewish and non-Jewish judges were asked to sort images into the category "Jewish" and "non-Jewish."[24] Jews had a greater ability to identify "Jewish" photographs, as did non-Jewish judges who showed a higher index for anti-Semitism. Was it that these two groups were more closely attuned to the subliminal signs of Jewishness, or was it that they simply judged more of the images to be Jewish? The former seemed to be the case.[25] Jewish judges "tended to give more false positives and were more accurate than non-Jews." The conclusion was that they "were particularly sensitive to possible cues in others which would enable them to ascribe group membership to these others and that this disposition was directly related to the degree of acceptance of the majority stereotype."[26] One could add: even if the subjects were believed to be hiding their Jewishness. What was being measured was the anxious perception of a "Jewish" physiognomy. Non-Jewish as well as Jewish participants identified Jewish images as Jewish more than 30 percent of the time. This exceeded their identification as Jewish when the experimenters supplied speech, gesture, and name. Neither sports nor sweets made the Jew into an "American" in the 1940s.

Gay's America is the land of boundless opportunities, at least for successful Jews of the Kissinger generation. (And the unsuccessful ones don't write their memoirs.) Gay's autobiography provides a powerful argument for reordering our sense of German American texts and expanding them to include those written by Jews and written in English. Here the borderland of the field becomes more complex and difficult to discern. Which is exactly why scholarship should be brought to bear examining it!

Teaching and writing across the disciplines means showing students and readers how parts of a culture are related, in complex and often unusual ways, to other seemingly remote aspects of a culture. My teaching in medical school settings has often meant trying to relate the world of cutting-edge science to concerns for meaning and context. When Dolly, the first cloned mammal, appeared on the horizon, she presented a new set of problems and options for teaching the culture of medicine. Dolly changed the way I (and virtually everyone else) thought about the potential for medicine in the next millennium.

In the third week of February 1997, it was announced that Ian

Wilmut, working in a private Scottish laboratory, had cloned a lamb from a cell of an adult sheep. She was named Dolly after the buxom country-music star Dolly Parton, because the cell came from the mother's udder (the first true "breast implant!").[1] The project was to create offspring from an adult cell that would carry the unchanged genetic line of the parent. The appearance of a true mammalian clone (whose genetic makeup could potentially live forever) and the radical response to Dolly set me to thinking.

What struck me in the first responses to the appearance of Dolly was that their visions of the future looked very much like the past—specifically like the Third Reich. Over and over again commentators invoked Ira Levin's novel *The Boys from Brazil* and Franklin J. Schaffner's 1978 film version, with Gregory Peck, Laurence Olivier, James Mason, Lilli Palmer, and Steve Guttenberg. In the novel and film, latter-day Nazis, under the direction of the mad Nazi scientist Josef Mengele, unsuccessfully conspire to produce 94 clones of Adolf Hitler.[2] The cloning would provide the potential to rejuvenate the Nazis and their world. Yet it fails precisely because the fictive clones have lives of their own. None of them can become Hitler because none has had childhood experiences identical to his. Surely this was an oddly negative model to invoke to examine the potential of human cloning.

Dolly's existence raised a series of concerns that were virtually all articulated through the fear of resurrected Nazism. Thus Patrick Dixon, an expert in the ethics of genetic engineering, called the clone "a Frankenstein's monster and a short step from Hitler's dream of creating a master race."[3] Dixon warned of "the dangers of human clones — like the plot of the film *The Boys from Brazil* in which boy copies of Hitler are created from one of his hairs." He added: "Imagine what Hitler would have done if he had access to this technology. By the end of the war, there could have been 50 to 100 children who were the image of Hitler."

One can also imagine (as I write this) that the entire force of science could be turned to the reproduction of younger copies of ourselves. Not merely the joy of the continuation of the "race," but the ultimate fantasy of the eugenic manipulators—a perfect world of perfect people. Each person could be remade not merely in his or her own image but as a perfect younger self. As Robert Coles has noted, "It tempts our narcissism enormously because it gives a physical dimension to a fantasy that one can keep going on through the reproduction of oneself."[4] And this is a fantasy of rejuvenation, with all of the Faustian echoes— remaining eternally young by recreating oneself as one's own child.

And yet the problem of cloning is indeed closely con- nected to the biology of race and the concerns of the Third Reich. Wilmut's success came after a long series of attempts to create identical mammals. The first practical model was suggested in 1938 by the German embryologist Hans Spe- mann (1869–1941), who is often called the father of mod- ern embryology.[5] Working in Nazi Germany, with its fan- tasies of breeding a master race, he proposed what he called a "fantastical experiment": to remove the nucleus from an egg cell and put into its place a nucleus from another cell. The problem proved intractable: it was only in 1952 that two American scientists, Robert Briggs and T. J. King, used very fine pipettes to suck the nucleus out of a frog egg and replace it with the nucleus of a cell from an adult frog. Eighteen years later the British developmental biologist John Gurdon inserted nuclei from advanced toad embryos rather than from adult tissue. The toad eggs developed into tadpoles but died before becoming adults. In 1984, Steen Willadsen, a Danish embryologist working in Texas, succeeded in cloning a sheep using a nucleus from a cell of an early embryo. Wilmut, by using a cell from a fully grown animal, was the first to fulfill the Western fantasy of the "real" clone: the youthful replication of the adult self.

Why is it that cloning caused such a scare in the press and in discussions about the future? What is it about cloning that frightens as well as attracts? The answer, of course, lies in its apparent promise of the chance to live forever. That is the desire underlying our dutiful consumption of broccoli and other antioxidants, our rejection of beef, ice cream, and tobacco, and our determination to run, run, run. We do these things not merely for our health but because we wish to cut a deal with the Creator. "Listen, God," we pray. "If I sacrifice things I love, will you let me live forever?" Now cloning provides us with that possibility.

Early examples in American literature warn against the hubris of such deal-making. Two nineteenth-century tales by Nathaniel Hawthorne present the transformation of the body as corrosive and as destructive. "Dr. Heidegger's Experiment" (1837) recounts an attempt to rejuvenate the body with water from the Fountain of Youth that goes horribly wrong.[6] Dr. Heidegger invites four "melancholy old creatures," including a woman who "was a great beauty in her day," to drink water from the Fountain of Youth. The water first revives a pale, dried flower, whose color turns "a deepening tinge of crimson." The crimson of the flower, like the crimson of the birthmark, is a sign of the vitality of blood. When the four try the water, they gradually become younger, and the old eroticism which bound the three men in the story to the woman reappears. The "gray, decrepit, sapless, miserable creatures" become "young!" The woman looks into a mirror "to see whether some long-remembered wrinkle or crow's-foot had indeed vanished." All of them leap about the room and dance, knocking over the carafe of water, and begin again to age. The lesson learned by the doctor who watches them is that youth is a poor substitute for the wisdom of age, but the four friends go off nevertheless to search for the Fountain of Youth.

Hawthorne's story "The Birth-Mark" (1846) reflects the failure of an aesthetic procedure to alter the body satisfactorily. The obsessive attention by the husband to his wife's facial imperfection, a birthmark, causes her death. His eventual cure is a tincture of the "Elixir of Immortality, . . . a liquid that should prolong life for years—perhaps interminably—but that . . . would produce a discord in nature, which all the world, and chiefly the quaffer of the immortal nostrum, would find cause to curse." The tincture lightens the "crimson mark," but the lighter the birthmark grows, the more feeble his wife becomes, and eventually she dies. Hawthorne condemns both rejuvenation and aesthetic surgery as failures, playing on older Faustian notions of the necessary failure of both rejuvenation and reconstruction to make the human being happy.[7] And, as we know, Faust's bargain is a devilish one, which he escapes only because of supernatural (if not Divine) intercession. His rejuvenation is a sign of his failure.

The cloning of human beings provides the promise and illusion of eternal life. The next century will see an expanding number of centenarians: the population will live longer, if not better. The prospect of perpetual youth and the anxieties it engenders are a persistent part of Western culture after the Shoah. Aldous Huxley (1894–1963) peoples his novel *Brave New World* (1946) with individuals developed through embryo splitting (called "bokanovskification"). Huxley draws on the Nazi desire (and attempt) to create a new race of Germans in their *Lebensborn*, the breeding ground of the master race, and in the thought experiments of their biologists. Taking these one step further, Huxley imagines a world in which there are classes of eternally young people, one always replacing another. He separated his Gammas, Deltas, and Epsilons from the higher-class Alphas and Betas not just by economic status but also by biologically engineered physical and intellectual traits. This world is inhabited by identical people who remain young forever, since they are replaced with identical copies as they age. Such a world exists based on the very concept of perpetual rejuvenation as a form of slavery. Woody Allen's parody of this tradition of the dangerous clone in *Sleeper* (1973) has him kidnapping the severed nose of a Big Brother–like dictator before it can be cloned to oppress the world once more. Politics and cloning come to be related in a magical way, as they are in Huxley's novel. The experiences of the Third Reich are a sublimated part of all modern discourses on cloning and rejuvenation.

Yet the image of the eternally young and healthy self is a fantasy that we all share to ward off the fear of mortality. Medicine can promise us neither immortality nor even that wonderful fantasy of the eighteenth century, the "good death." The other discussion that has haunted me lately is that of euthanasia. The anxiety about it, evoking the same vocabulary of Nazi atrocities and the Shoah, is the other side of the cloning debate. If we can, through our clones, live forever, each organism must at some point be made to die.

Can we live forever? And, if not, how will we die? At the end of the millennium, with its symbolic evocation of ends and beginnings, these two questions haunt us. Assuredly we can live forever, but not through medicine. I, as a teacher, stand in a long tradition of immortality. In 1997 archeologists uncovered the ruins of Aristotle's Lyceum, the school where he taught philosophy to the elite of Athens. Education too is a form of cloning, but one that permits radical change over time. Individual immortality is neither possible nor desirable, but the need to function as educated men and women in a world such as that of higher education makes us part of an immortal undertaking, part of a long chain not of genes but of knowledge. Not merely copies of the past, but new and exciting participants in the present, and shapers and molders of the future. Possessors of the past, creators of a brave new future—students stand both as our products and as the revolutionaries who overturn our past. Can we live forever? I certainly shall—through the students who will carry on my mission, that of educating a new world, either in my own ideals or in theirs.

NOTES

Chapter One

1. *German Quarterly* 62 (1989):192–204.

2. Two German-language texts already exist: Jost Hermand's *Als Pimpf in Polen* (Frankfurt: Fischer, 1993), his autobiography of his youth under the Nazis, and Ruth Klüger's *Weiter Leben* (Göttingen: Wallstein, 1992). Both could serve as models for addressing our post-Shoah, American experiences as Germanists.

Chapter Two

1. *Building a National Literature: The Case of Germany 1830–1870* (Ithaca: Cornell University Press, 1989). Hohendahl posits the rise of literary criticism as a means of political identity formation.

Chapter Four

1. *Chronicle of Higher Education*, December 15, 1995.

2. Cary Nelson, "Lessons from the Job Wars: What Is to Be Done?" *Academe* 81 (November–December 1995): 18–25.

Chapter Seven

1. John T. Krumpelmann, *Bayard Taylor and German Letters* (Hamburg: Cram/De Gruyter, 1959).

2. John T. Krumpelmann, *Southern Scholars in Goethe's*

Germany (Chapel Hill: University of North Carolina Press, 1965).

3. Heinz Kindermann, ed., *Rufe über Grenzen: Antlitz und Lebenstraum der Grenz- und Auslanddeutschen in ihrer Dichtung* (Berlin: Junge Generation Verlag, 1938).

4. Here one can mention W. G. Sebald's work on recent Austrian writing, *Unheimliche Heimat* (Salzburg: Residenz, 1991).

5. Walter D. Kamphoefer, Wolfgang Helbig, and Ulrike Sommer, eds., *News from the Land of Freedom: German Immigrants Write Home*, translated by Susan Vogel (Ithaca: Cornell University Press, 1993).

6. Linda Schelbitzki Pickle, *Contented among Strangers: Rural German-Speaking Women and Their Families in the Nineteenth-Century Midwest* (Urbana: University of Illinois Press, 1996).

7. Carol J. Poore, *German-American Socialist Literature, 1865–1900* (Bern: P. Lang, 1982).

8. Karl J. R. Arndt, *The German Language Press of the Americas, 1732–1968: History and Bibliography* (Pullach/München: Verlag Dokumentation, 1973).

9. Kathleen Neils Conzen, *Immigrant Milwaukee, 1836–1860: Accommodation and Community in a Frontier City* (Cambridge: Harvard University Press, 1976).

10. Ursula Hegi, *Tearing the Silence: On Being German in America* (New York: Simon and Schuster, 1997).

11. This theme is also echoed in complex ways in a recent essay by Sabine Gölz, "How Ethnic Am I?" *PMLA* 113 (1998): 46–51.

12. Björn Krondorfer, *Remembrance and Reconciliation: Encounters between Young Jews and Germans* (New Haven: Yale University Press, 1995).

13. Ruth Klüger, *Weiter Leben* (Göttingen: Wallstein, 1992).

14. Timothy J. Holian, *The German-Americans and World War II: An Ethnic Experience* (New York: Lang, 1996), and Don Heinrich Tolzmann, ed., *German Americans in the World Wars*, vol. 4, *The World War II Experience: The Internment of German-Americans* (Munich: Sauer, 1995).

15. See the review by Jeffrey Sammons, "Were German-Americans Interned during World War II?" *German Quarterly* 71.1 (Winter 1998): 73–77, here 77n4.

16. Stephen Aron, "Lessons in Conquest: Towards a Greater Western History," *Pacific Historical Review* 63 (1991): 125–47, here 128.

17. Kerwin Lee Klein, "Reclaiming the 'F' Word, or Being and Becoming Postwestern," *Pacific Historical Review* 65 (1996): 179–215.

18. Gloria Anzaldúa, *Borderlands/La Frontera: The New Mestiza* (San Francisco: Spinsters/Aunt Lute, 1987), 79–81.

19. Richard White, *The Middle Ground: Indians, Empires, and Republics in the Great Lakes Region, 1650–1815* (Cambridge: Cambridge University Press, 1991).

20. The term is from Dan Diner, "Negative Symbiose: Deutsche und Juden nach Auschwitz," *Babylon* 1 (1986): 9–20. On its applicability in the present context see Jack Zipes, "Die kulturellen Operation von Deutschen und Juden im Spiegel der neueren deutschen Literatur," *Babylon* 8 (1990): 34–44; Klaus Briegleb, "Negative Symbiose," in Klaus Briegleb and Sigrid Weigel, eds., *Gegenwartsliteratur seit 1968* (Munich: Hanser, 1992), 117–52; Hans Schütz, *Juden in der deutschen Literatur* (Munich: Piper, 1992), 309–29.

21. Part of this difference is due to the very early Germanization (or Magyarization) of the Jews in their modern history (as opposed to the marginal Polinization or

Russification of most Jews, which did not occur until the early twentieth century).

22. Peter Fröhlich, *My German Question: Growing Up in Nazi Berlin* (New Haven: Yale University Press, 1998).

23. Jacob Wassermann, *My Life as German and Jew* (London: George Allen & Unwin, 1933), 156.

24. Gordon Allport and Bernard M. Kramer, "Some Roots of Prejudice," *Journal of Psychology* 22 (1946): 9–39. See also Frederick H. Lund and Wilner C. Berg, "Identifiability of Nationality Characteristics," *Journal of Social Psychology* 24 (1946): 77–83; Launor F. Carter, "The Identification of 'Racial' Membership," *Journal of Abnormal and Social Psychology* 43 (1948): 279–86; Gardner Lindzey and Saul Rogolsky, "Prejudice and Identification of Minority Group Membership," *Journal of Abnormal and Social Psychology* 45 (1950): 37–53; and Donald N. Elliott and Bernard H. Wittenberg, "Accuracy of Identification of Jewish and Non-Jewish Photographs," *Journal of Abnormal and Social Psychology* 51 (1955): 339–41.

25. Leonard D. Savitz and Richard F. Tomasson, "The Identifiability of Jews," *American Journal of Sociology* 64 (1958): 468–75.

26. Alvin Scodel and Harvey Austrin, "The Perception of Jewish Photographs by Non-Jews and Jews," *Journal of Abnormal and Social Psychology* 54 (1957): 278–80.

Chapter Eight

1. George B. Johnson, "One Small Step for Man: A Giant Leap with a Sheep," *St. Louis Post-Dispatch*, March 20, 1997, 01G.

2. Ira Levin, *The Boys from Brazil* (New York: Random House, 1976).

3. Ian Dow, "Is Dolly the First Step to Creating a Master Race? Fears of Nazi-Style Master Race Experiments over New Cloned Sheep," *Daily Record*, February 24, 1997, 8.

4. Gustav Niebuhr, "Suddenly, Religious Ethicists Face a Quandary on Cloning," *New York Times*, March 1, 1997, A1.

5. Otto Mangold, *Hans Spemann, ein Meister der Entwicklungsphysiologie, sein Leben und sein Werk* (Stuttgart: Wissenschaftlich Verlagsgesellschaft, 1953).

6. All quotes are from Nathaniel Hawthorne, *Tales and Sketches* (New York: Library of America, 1982): "Dr. Heidegger's Experiment," 470–79; and "The Birth-Mark," 764–80.

7. Marie Mulvey Roberts, "'A Physic against Death': Eternal Life and the Enlightenment—Gender and Gerontology," *Literature and Medicine during the Eighteenth Century*, eds. Marie Mulvey Roberts and Roy Porter (London: Routledge, 1993), 151–67.

Library of Congress Cataloging-in-Publication Data

Gilman, Sander L.
  The fortunes of the humanities : thoughts for after the year 2000 /
Sander L. Gilman
      p.   cm.
  ISBN 0-8047-3263-9 (cloth : alk. paper)—
  ISBN 0-8047-3264-7 (paper : alk. paper)
  Includes bibliographical references.
      1. Humanities—Study and teaching (Higher)—United States.
  2. Humanities—Philosophy.   3. Learning and scholarship—
  United States—History.   I. Title.
  AZ183.U5G55   2000
  001.3'071'173—dc21   00-041054

  ∞   This book is printed on acid-free, recycled paper.

Original printing 2000
Last figure below indicates year of this printing:
09   08   07   06   05   04   03   02   01   00

Designed by James P. Brommer
Typeset in 11/15 Bembo and Futura